The Asbury Theologi͟ ͟ ͟ ͟ ͟ ͟ ͟ ͟ ͟ ͟ ͟ ͟ ͟y ͟ ͟ ͟ ͟ ͟ ͟ ͟ ͟ ͟ ͟ ͟ ͟ ͟ ͟ ͟ in
Christian Revitalization Studies

MW01256197

This volume is published in collaboration with the Asbury Theological Seminary Series in Christian Revitalization Studies, and appears in its Systematic Theology and Philosophy section. Building on the work of the previous Wesleyan/Holiness Studies Center at the Seminary, the Series provides a focus for research in the Wesleyan Holiness and other related Christian renewal movements, including Pietism and Pentecostal movements, which have had a world impact. The research seeks to develop analytical models of these movements, including their biblical and theological assessment. Using an interdisciplinary approach, the Series bridges relevant discourses in several areas in order to gain insights for effective Christian mission globally. It recognizes the need for conducting research that combines insights from the history of evangelical renewal and revival movements with anthropological and religious studies literature on revitalization movements.

Among the many volumes published in this Series, we now offer one which addresses the fundamental question of why theological inquiry is important, not only for seminary students, but for everyone who has asked the deeper questions of what is the meaning and purpose of human life, and yours or mine in particular. In brief, it is a lucid account of how the discipline of theology, understood from its biblical basis, offers satisfying and challenging answers to these important questions, reflecting a variety of theological disciplines. The publication here of *An Invitation to Theology*, presented in a day when a secularized society would triumphantly view itself as representing a post Christian world, is timely and needed, even beyond the scope of this Series, in which it appears. Indeed, its relevance and poignancy strikes at the heart of what a Series devoted to the study of Christian revitalization movements is about.

J. Steven O'Malley, General Editor
The Asbury Theological Seminary Studies in Christian Revitalization

Sub-Series in Philosophical/Systematic Theology

The purpose of this sub-series in Philosophical/Systematic Theology is to make available the results of recent scholarly research into the various issues that have relevance for the revitalization of Christian thinking and spiritual formation in the life of the Church.

This book is scholarly written and designed primarily for university and seminary students who are beginning to read seriously about the nature of Christian theology. Students who do not have the opportunity to study theology in a formal setting but who take seriously a thoughtful understanding of Christian faith will also find this work accessible and invaluable. This book provides a summary of the basic ideas of what Christians believe and why they believe them. We are living in an unprecedented period of time of pluralistic thinking when Christian believers must know why they believe in Jesus Christ. This work is a friendly invitation to consider the importance and the truthfulness of Christian belief.

Laurence W. Wood
Subseries Editor
Frank Paul Morris Professor of Systematic Theology
Asbury Theological Seminary

For Love of God

An Invitation to Theology

Ronnie P. Campbell Jr.

The Asbury Theological Seminary Series in Philosophical/Systematic Theology

EMETH PRESS
www.emethpress.com

For Love of God
An Invitation to Theology
Copyright © 2017 Ronnie P. Campbell Jr.

Library of Congress Cataloging-in-Publication Data

Names: Campbell, Ronnie P., author.
Title: For love of God : an invitation to theology / Ronnie P. Campbell Jr.
Description: Lexington : Emeth Press, 2017. | Includes bibliographical
    references.
Identifiers: LCCN 2017047895 | ISBN 9781609471200 (alk. paper)
Subjects: LCSH: Theology.
Classification: LCC BR118 .C233 2017 | DDC 230--dc23
LC record available at https://lccn.loc.gov/2017047895

To Debbie

I am grateful to the Lord for your love and friendship.

Table of Contents

Acknowledgements / ix

Introduction / xi

Chapter 1 Theologizing Everything / 1

Chapter 2 Shaping a Worldview / 15

Chapter 3 Defending the Hope Within / 31

Chapter 4 Correcting False Teaching / 45

Chapter 5 Removing Doubt / 65

Chapter 6 Becoming Living Sacrifices / 77

Chapter 7 Building Character / 85

Chapter 8 Making Disciples / 101

Chapter 9 Growing in Worship / 109

Chapter 10 Integrating Faith / 115

Selected Bibliography / 127

Acknowledgements

The writing of a book is never a solo act. Teachers are learners, and we in the academy share with others what has been handed down to us. Far too many people contributed to my own learning and formation that can be mentioned in this book. But one teacher stands above the rest. Thank you, Mark Eckel, for investing in me as a young student at the Moody Bible Institute. Many of my own ideas and thoughts about theology and the integration of faith and learning began in your classroom. At times it is difficult to tell where your thoughts end and mine begin. I did my best to attribute those thoughts to you when due, but as you know, the student is often the extension of his teacher. Brother. Teacher. Friend.

I would also like to thank my colleagues at Liberty University: Chad Thornhill, who read copies of my initial chapters; Ben Forrest, who spurred me on to complete this project; and David Baggett, who remained an immutable source of encouragement and inspiration to this young academic. In addition, I would like to thank Ed Hindson, the dean of the Rawlings School of Divinity at Liberty University, for his leadership and dedication to scholarly theological training and Christ-centered practical ministry.

To my students, Adam Morrone and Cooper Ramsey, who read through an earlier draft of this book, your comments were invaluable. Thank you! I teach because of students like you.

Nate Isidro, Todd Smith, and Josh Waltman, your constant encouragement and persistent friendship are good gifts from God.

Finally, I want to thank Debbie, Abby, Caedmon, Caleb, and Zeke. Each day you remind me of God's goodness. I can think of no one else with whom I would rather do life, theology, and pizza night.

Introduction

Questions come in all shapes and sizes, and some are more difficult to answer than others. Generally, the hardest questions start with "why." Asking "why" causes us to look deep within our souls, search hard, and find purpose in what we're doing. This book wrestles with an important "why" question: *Why should anyone care about, let alone study, theology?*

This book has a specific audience in mind: college students at Christian colleges and universities, who are required to take introductory theology courses, but who have had little or no exposure to theology. Seminarians may also find this book useful as a preface to their Seminary studies, especially those who come from an academic background outside of religious studies or theology.

Having taught college students for over a decade, I've found that students enjoy theology but want to know what kind of practical relevance it has for their lives. Why does it matter if I study theology or not? What does theology have to do with my discipline or chosen vocation? These questions form the heart of this work.

This book, then, isn't about theological method, nor is it a theological treatise or textbook; rather, it is *an invitation to study theology*, aimed at helping students of all disciplines—not just theology, pastoral, or religion majors—to see the practical relevance of theology to their lives. While most theology textbooks comment on the importance of studying theology, such attempts are often brief and cursory. *For Love of God* provides students with a framework for understanding how the study of theology can impact their lives in a deeper way.

Though aimed at college students and beginning Seminarians, this book should not be limited to those within the academy. *For Love of God* has been written in such a way that it is accessible to those without formal theological training, and, therefore, can be a valuable tool for pastors, lay leaders, adult Bible study teachers, and anyone who is interested in learning about theology.

The book's layout is straightforward. Each chapter corresponds to a reason for studying theology:

Reason 1: Theologizing Everything

Reason 2: Shaping a Worldview

Reason 3: Defending the Hope Within

Reason 4: Correcting False Teaching

Reason 5: Removing Doubt

Reason 6: Becoming Living Sacrifices

Reason 7: Building Character

Reason 8: Making Disciples

Reason 9: Growing in Worship

Reason 10: Integrating Faith

These chapters taken together focus on how theology influences our practices, character, personal interactions, engagement with culture, choice of vocation, evangelism, and love for God. Chapter one sets the stage by highlighting two key principles: (1) everything is theological and (2) all truth is God's truth. Chapter two builds a biblical case for Christians knowing what they believe and why, which forms the backbone for the rest of the book. Chapters three through five are apologetically oriented, emphasizing theology's role in defending the faith (chapter 3), warding off false teaching (chapter 4), and removing doubt (chapter 5); whereas chapters six through nine focus on spiritual formation (chapters 6-7), evangelism and discipleship (chapter 8), and a life of worship (chapter 9). The final chapter—chapter ten—takes up the challenge of helping students integrate their faith into daily practice. It places focus on key principles for integration, offering examples of how such theological principles may be integrated into various disciplines.

Chapter One

Theologizing Everything

What's Wrong with Theology?

The-ol-o-gy. Why should anyone care about, let alone study, this four-syllable word? I remember hearing a song in high school proclaiming that we didn't need theology to know that God is good to us. Unfortunately, the words of that song are contradictory. "God is good" is itself a theological statement! Now, by this, the artists might simply have meant that one doesn't need to study theology to know that God is good to His people, or they may have meant that one doesn't need to take a course in theology to know that God is good to us. That very well may be true, but as it stands, the statement is ambiguous. But even if the author had one of the other meanings in mind, it still reflects a trend within American evangelicalism that somehow theology isn't needed.

To see this trend, all one needs to do is visit the local Christian bookstore and compare the theology section with the self-help and practical living sections. Most Christian bookstores (outside of the university) that I've visited have one or two shelves dedicated to theology, if that. (Surprisingly, my local Barnes and Noble has a larger theology section than some Christian bookstores I've seen.) On top of this, look to our churches. Worship lyrics focus more on our response than on the God to whom we're responding. Sermons and Bible studies center on practical application, without diving deep into the core doctrines of the Christian faith. When doctrine is touched on, it's often done in a cursory way. Why is it that so many Christians are reluctant to study theology? One could list a myriad of reasons, but I'll consider three strands of thought: intellectual enterprise, heart vs. head, and anti-intellectualism.

Intellectual Enterprise. Some Christians see theology as something people do when they have too much time on their hands, or as something for pastors and academics, not the common person on the street. It's nothing more than a leisurely intellectual enterprise that people get into squabbles about. Sadly, people do get into heated discussions on theological topics at times. Anyone who's ever been around a Calvinist and Arminian going at it over God's sovereignty and the nature of human freedom knows just how quickly the discussion can escalate. You would think Mt. St. Helens had erupted or a nuclear power plant was going critical. But if theology is merely an intellectual pursuit, then we're missing the point.

The English word "theology" is comprised of two Greek words, *theos* (God) and *logos* (study, word, or discourse on). Simply put, theology means "the study of God" or "a discourse on God." When we focus our study on God's personhood, nature, and attributes, we're doing theology in the *narrow* sense of the word. But most theologians and theological works recognize theology to be more expansive than that, covering all points of Christian teaching. Theology in the *broad* sense of the word covers not only God's personhood, nature, and attributes, but expands to God's workings in the world, the nature of His creatures, and their response to Him.[1] As we'll see below, if Christians are right and God is the creator of all things, then, as God's creatures, we're ultimately responsible to Him. All of our thoughts, attitudes, and actions stand before the Creator of all things.

You might be saying, "that's all well, good, and fine, but what's the purpose of theology?" First and foremost, theology is an activity of the church and not merely that of the academy. The task of theology has always been caught up in the life and mission of the church. Some of the greatest theologians during the first four centuries of the Christian movement (and afterwards, too!) were also pastors. These pastor-theologians understood that central to the life and heartbeat of the church is God's revelation (self-disclosure or unveiling) to us—the Bible. For in it we find purpose, meaning, and mission. They fought rigorously to defend its core teachings (doctrine) against attacks from false teachers. There's much we can learn from them. As a people of the book, we cannot do theology apart from the Bible. The Bible, as the source of God's special revelation (i.e., knowledge about God and His purposes that we could not have arrived at on our own through reason or observation of nature), provides the raw data by which we practice and engage in the task of theologizing. It provides the framework for our thinking, shaping our beliefs, so that we can respond appropriately to God and engage the world at large.

Theology, then, is concerned not only with having correct beliefs about God, but also with having a proper response to our Creator. On the one hand, theology requires rigorous study. It requires both the collection and organization of data from Scripture and then thinking hard about how interpretations of the data explain our world and reality itself. There is a science to it—*scientia*. The aim is to come to correct beliefs about God, our world, and His interactions in it. On the other hand, theology is concerned with godly living, or as the ancients called it, "wisdom"—*sapientia*.[2] In summarizing Augustine's thought on theology as the pursuit of wisdom, David Clark writes:

> Augustine's notion that Christians should direct their knowing to the highest good, namely, the wisdom of God, is still a legitimate contemporary use of the word 'wis-

---

[1] Henry C. Thiessen, *Lectures in Systematic Theology*, rev. by Vernon D. Doerksen (1979; repr., Grand Rapids, MI: William B. Eerdmans, 2000), 1-2.

[2] David K. Clark, *To Know and Love God* (Wheaton, IL: Crossway Books, 2003), 208-219.

dom'. In this sense, godly wisdom is knowledge directed to salvation and Christian living. Wisdom is not merely knowing *about* God, but understanding directed toward knowing God personally.[3]

As those seeking to do theology, our ultimate goal is to know and love God and to bring Him glory in all that we do.

Heart vs. Head. Some people want to pit *scientia* against *sapientia.* This kind of thinking is often called "heart-knowledge" verses "head-knowledge." But it's not enough, however, to have *sapientia* without *scientia.* Both are needed. An analogy may help to flesh this out. Anyone who has ever owned a computer knows that every so often its programs need updates in order to function efficiently and properly. Without these updates, the program might not run or it runs in a quirky way. Here's a personal example to drive this point home. My wife and I have opted out of having cable or satellite in our house. We prefer to watch T.V. shows online through our computer. There have been times that we've tried to watch a show, only to find out that our computer didn't have the latest update needed, and therefore we could not stream the show. That, I suggest, is often how it is in life. There are times that we need to update our beliefs to function in life as God intended.

Granted, like all analogies, this one, too, breaks down. As God's human creatures, made in the image and likeness of God, we are not meat-machines or fleshy-computer-processors. Our brains (or minds) and nervous systems aren't created to merely receive and process data. There is a creative element to our thinking. Nevertheless, there are times when we lack knowledge. Our beliefs are insufficient or underdeveloped, and this can affect how we live our lives (as we'll see below). There's *an incompleteness* to our understanding of the world. What else might we expect as finite human beings? We are not all-knowing (omniscient) like God. This incompleteness in knowledge is, in part, what separates us from God. He is uncreated; we are created. He is infinite; we are finite. He is immortal; we are mortal. He is all-powerful; we are limited in power. He depends on nothing; we are dependent on Him for our very existence. This is what theologians call "the Creator/creature distinction." Yet, such an incompleteness also sets us apart from the beasts. Our learning is not merely instinctual. We don't merely live by desire and appetite. We *can* grow in our knowledge and understanding of God and His world. We can stand in awe of sunsets, discover the mysteries of our world and the universe, and have personal knowledge of our grand Creator—something the beasts can never do.

You might be thinking, "Indeed, God has given us the capacity to know and understand Him and His good world, but shouldn't Christians place more emphasis on how they live instead of on what they know? Or, to put it another way, shouldn't we be more concerned with our hearts and actions than with our heads?"

From personal observation of various churches that I've attended, Sunday morning sermons and weekly Bible studies often focus on practical living, which isn't itself a bad thing. After all, as Christians we are called to live a life of obedi-

---

[3]Ibid., 208.

ence, righteousness, and holiness (Mt 6:33; John 14:23; 1 Pt 1:15-16). The problem, however, is that our beliefs impact our attitudes and behaviors. As the old
saying goes, "Ideas have legs."

To grasp this more clearly, let's take our computer analogy even further. If a
computer obtains a virus, it corrupts or deletes data, which causes the computer to
malfunction. False beliefs about God, creation, and His human creatures are like
computer viruses, corrupting how we function in God's good world. False beliefs
lead to all kinds of disastrous effects. Doubt, worry, anxiety, false teaching, sin,
wrong attitudes, bad relationships, self-loathing, abuse of animals, destruction of
the earth, and even death all come about from skewed thinking.

Several years ago, anxiety came knocking at my door. It was one of the dark-
est periods of my life. Feelings of being overwhelmed filled my every thought.
The more I thought about what I had to do with my work, the less I accomplished.
Like a vehicle caught in the mud, my mental wheels were spinning and I was going nowhere. Not only did my anxiety affect me, but it also affected various other
relationships I had, whether in the family, at work, or in the church. To make a
long story short, the root behind much of my anxiety stemmed from false beliefs.
A vital part of getting over my anxiety included removing those false beliefs and
replacing them with truth. False beliefs often destroy the vitality of our faith.

But there is another way that false beliefs affect us. Sometimes they clutter
our thinking. Again, let us turn to our computer analogy for clarification. For
computers to run optimally, not only must its systems be clear of viruses and
all programs properly updated, but sometimes unwanted programs slow down
processing and take up space. To maximize speed, these unnecessary programs
should be removed. In a similar way, we live in a culture of competing worldviews and ideologies. We are constantly bombarded with ideas, whether from our
news channels, social media, classrooms, or friends. Knowing what we believe
and why helps us to navigate life with greater clarity. That doesn't mean that we'll
always have the right answers, nor does it mean that decisions won't be difficult at
times. Rather, knowing what it is we believe and why we believe it will enable us
to make informed decisions that are both morally and practically honoring to God.

Ultimately, pitting head against heart commits the either/or fallacy, that is,
such thinking suggests that God is primarily concerned with our hearts or that
God is primarily concerned with our heads. Jesus put it to us like this: we are to
love God with all that we have—heart, soul, mind, and strength (Matt 22:37; Lk
10:27)![4]

Anti-intellectualism. Much of theology's rejection stems from the rampant
anti-intellectualism taking place, not only within our churches, but also in society at large. Such anti-intellectualism has far-reaching effects. In an important,
but chilling, address given at Wheaton College, Charles Malik warns that "the

---

[4]For an excellent work on the importance of reason in our lives, see *J. P. Moreland:
Love Your God with All Your Mind: The Role of Reason in the Life of the Soul* (Colorado
Springs, CO: NavPress, 1997).

greatest danger besetting American evangelical Christianity is the danger of anti-intellectualism."[5] He continues:

> The mind as to its greatest and deepest reaches is not cared for enough. This cannot take place apart from profound immersion for a period of years in the history of thought and the spirit. People are in a hurry to get out of the university and start earning money or serving the Church or preaching the gospel. They have no idea of the infinite value of spending years of leisure in conversing with the greatest minds and souls of the past and thereby ripening and sharpening and enlarging their powers of thinking. The result is that the arena of creative thinking is abdicated and vacated to the enemy. Who among evangelicals can stand up to the great secular or naturalistic or atheistic scholars on their own terms of scholarship and research? Who among evangelical scholars is quoted as a normative source by the greatest secular authorities on history or philosophy or psychology or sociology or politics? Does your mode of thinking have the slightest chance of becoming the dominant mode of thinking in the great universities of Europe and America, which stamp your entire civilization with their own spirit and ideas?[6]

Malik's warning is both challenging and sobering. He recognized that ideas are powerful and that as evangelical Christians we must care deeply for the mind. If we are not filling the slots and leading the way in our universities and institutions of higher learning, vocations, places of influence within society, and within our churches, then we are leaving vacant a watershed of non-Christian ideologies, which have already begun to infiltrate our society. Similarly, in an address to Christian philosophers, Alvin Plantinga warns of the pervasiveness of such non-Christian assumptions in our disciplines and charges Christians to "develop the right Christian alternatives."[7] He writes:

> First, it isn't just in philosophy that we Christians are heavily influenced by the practices and procedures of our non-Christian peers. . . . The same holds for nearly any important contemporary intellectual discipline: history, literary and artistic criticism, musicology, and the sciences, both social and natural. In all of these areas there are ways of proceeding, pervasive assumptions about the nature of the discipline. . . . But in many cases these assumptions and presumptions do not easily mesh with a Christian or theistic way of looking at the world . . . .. Christians must display autonomy and integrity. If contemporary mechanistic biology really has no place for human freedom, then something other than contemporary mechanistic biology is called for; and the Christian community must develop it. If contemporary psychology is fundamentally naturalist, then it is up to Christian psychologists to develop an alternative that fits well with Christian supernaturalism—one that takes its start from such scientifically seminal truths as that God has created humankind in his own image.[8]

---

[5]Charles Malik, "The Two Tasks." *Journal of the Evangelical Theological Society* 23, no. 4 (December 1980): 294.

[6]Ibid., 295.

[7]Alvin Plantinga, "Advice to Christian Philosophers: Preface," reprinted from *Faith and Philosophy: Journal of the Society of Christian Philosophers* 1, no. 3 (October 1984), 253-271, accessed July 9, 2016, http://www. faithandphilosophy.com/article_advice.php

[8]Ibid.

Christians ought to be leading the way not only in our disciplines, but in every sphere of life. In the words of the late Jerry Falwell, "If it's Christian, it ought to be better."

We must not be tempted here to see this as an "us" vs. "them" challenge, or that Christians are somehow better than others. We're all in need of God's grace, believer and unbeliever alike! Rather, it is a calling coming from deep within the wellsprings of the Christian worldview. All that we Christians do has a direction, a *telos*, an end goal, grounded in the mission and purposes of God's working in the world.

As those who belong to Christ, there is no room for complacency, whether in our home life, vocations, education, or engagement with culture. Jesus Christ is LORD! Jesus' lordship towers over all areas of life. No place is left unturned or untouched by it. As those who are committed to and under Christ's lordship, we are to "take every thought captive" (2 Cor 10:5) and do all that we do unto "the glory of God" (1 Cor 10:31). As the Psalmist declares,

¹ The earth is the LORD's and the fullness thereof,

the world and those who dwell therein,

² for he has founded it upon the seas

and established it upon the rivers.⁹

It is the Lord's because He is the one who created all things.

Everything Is Theological

From Christ's lordship emerges an important theological principle: *everything is theological*. Every decision we make. Every word we say. Every job that we take. Every thought we have. *Everything is theological because everything stands under the lordship of Christ*.

Most often when we think of theology, we have in mind the standard theological textbook categories, such as the study of God (theology proper), revelation (bibliology), humanity (theological anthropology), sin (hamartiology), salvation (soteriology), church (ecclesiology), and end times (eschatology). But theology extends to all categories and all disciplines, because God's dominion extends to all of life. Let's flesh this out a bit more.

Every person has, what Nicholas Wolterstorff calls, "control beliefs."[10] Control beliefs are such that they set the direction for other beliefs we have. We can imagine our beliefs fitting together in something like a web—let us call it a "web

---

⁹Unless otherwise noted, all quotations from Scripture are taken from the English Standard Version.

[10]Nicholas Wolterstorff, *Reason Within the Bounds of Religion*, 2nd ed reprint (Grand Rapids, MI: Wm. B. Eerdmans Publishing Co., 1999), 17.

of beliefs."[11] Found at the center of a person's web of beliefs are our most cherished beliefs, which set the pace for how the rest of the web turns out.

Perhaps, the most important control belief surrounds what we do with God. What a person does with God sets the foundation for all other beliefs that one has. This is not only true for Christians, but also for those who deny the existence of God (atheists, naturalists, and agnostics). After all, if there is no God, then all one is left with is nature (or, perhaps, abstract objects, as Platonists believe). It's natural processes all the way down—*ad infinitum*.

According to the naturalistic metanarrative, the universe exploded into existence some 13.8 billion years ago from out of the Big Bang, resulting in the formation of galaxies, stars, and planets, until eventually, through random evolutionary processes, life emerged from non-life out of a pre-biotic soup. In the words of philosopher J. P. Moreland,

> the process of evolution, understood in either neo-Darwinian or punctuated equilibrium terms, gave rise to all the life forms we see including human beings. Thus, all organisms and their parts exist and are what they are because they contributed to (or at least did not hinder) the struggle for reproductive advantage, more specifically, because they contributed to the tasks of feeding, fighting, fleeing, and reproducing.[12]

Such an understanding of life's emergence from natural, evolutionary processes has significant implications for one's understanding of humanity, ethics, and final hope. Life as we know it could have been quite different. Humans may never have evolved. Our being here is nothing more than a chance happening. But on top of that, as philosopher William Lane Craig argues, without the prospect of God or immortality, it seems life is absurd and *ultimately* without any hope. Craig explains,

> If God does not exist, life can be considered absurd. If there is no God, man inevitably is doomed to death. Like all biological organisms, he must die, and with no hope of immortality, his life leads no further than the grave. An individual's life is but a spark in the infinite blackness; it appears, flickers and dies forever. Compared to the infinite stretch of time, the span of a man's life is but an infinitesimal moment, and yet this is all the life he will ever know.[13]

Craig continues,

> The universe, too, faces death. Scientists tell us the universe is expanding, and everything in it is growing farther and farther apart. As it does so, it grows colder and colder, and its energy is used up. Eventually all the stars will burn out, and all matter will collapse into dead stars and black holes. There will be no light, no heat,

---

[11]By using the term "web of beliefs," I am not here advocating coherentism as a theory of truth; though I do find the concept of "web of beliefs" valuable in helping students see the interconnectedness between beliefs.

[12]J. P. Moreland, "The Ontological Status of Properties," in *Naturalism: A Critical Analysis*, eds. William Lane Craig and J. P. Moreland (New York: Routledge, 2000), 76.

[13]William Lane Craig, *The Existence of God and the Beginning of the Universe* (San Bernardino, CA: Here's Life Publishers, 1979), 13.

no life—only the corpses of dead stars and galaxies ever expanding into the endless darkness and the cold recesses of space, a universe in ruins.[14]

As with all biological life, the universe, too, ends in death. When it comes down to all our advances in knowledge, all our work to alleviate pain and suffering, and all of our efforts in making the world a better place, all of it ends with the universe. In such a world, Craig argues, there is no *ultimate* meaning, value, or purpose—life is absurd!

Christians, on the other hand, have a different metanarrative. Our story begins with God, the good Creator of all things, who created the heavens and the earth *ex nihilo*, that is, out of nothing (Gen 1:1, Jn 1:1-3; Col 1:15; Heb 1:2), *but not for nothing*. The creation has a goal and purpose behind it.

Coming out of the gates of the creation narrative of Genesis, we find that human beings were created in the image and likeness of God (Gen 1:26-27). It is because of this image that people have value, intrinsic worth, and rights (Gen 9:6; Jas 3:9). The narrative paints a vivid portrait of God's intimate working, care, and concern in the creation of our primordial ancestors (Gen 2:7). He fashioned and formed Adam from the stuff of the earth, and made Eve out from Adam's side. That same care with which He crafted His human creatures, God expects of them to show to the rest of His good creation. He charged them with the task of dominion as His vice regents over the garden and the rest of the world (Gen 1:28; 2:5, 15). The kind of dominion spoken of here is not that of oppression and violence, but of care and concern. They were to subdue the earth and bring it under God's rule and lordship.

The Christian metanarrative doesn't end with the creation account. Not too long into our grand story, we see the beginning stages of rebellion against God. Adam and Eve, whom God created to be His image bearers and called to have dominion over His creation, sinned and set humans in a downward spiral of broken relationships—broken relationships between God and humanity, one another, and the rest of creation.

But God doesn't leave it at that. The story of the Bible and of Christian theology is one where the Triune Creator God reaches down to a broken world, offering redemption, reconciliation, and re-creation. The book of Revelation paints a beautiful picture of what awaits us and our world:

> [1] Then I saw a new heaven and a new earth, for the first heaven and the first earth had passed away, and the sea was no more. [2] And I saw the holy city, new Jerusalem, coming down out of heaven from God, prepared as a bride adorned for her husband. [3] And I heard a loud voice from the throne saying, "Behold, the dwelling place of God is with man. He will dwell with them, and they will be his people, and God himself will be with them as their God. [4] He will wipe away every tear from their eyes, and death shall be no more, neither shall there be mourning, nor crying, nor pain anymore, for the former things have passed away." [5] And he who was seated on the throne said, "Behold, I am making all things new." (Rev 21:1-5)

---

[14]Ibid., 14.

God doesn't trash His creation; rather, He's in the process of making it new.

Reformed theologians have long understood the above shape to the Bible—creation, fall, and redemption.[15] At the center of the Christian metanarrative stands the work of the Triune God in bringing about a kingdom of peace and shalom, who is in the process of overthrowing the damaging effects of sin and restoring His good creation to His original intentions. Before moving on to our next principle, let's explore this three-fold shape a bit more.

The world that God created is a good world. Six times the Genesis narrative tells us that upon divine evaluation, God declared what He made as "good" (Gen 1:4, 10, 12, 18, 21, 25). On the seventh evaluation, at the completion of His human creatures, God declared it was "very good" (Gen 1:31). The problem, however, is now we live in a world that has been distorted by the effects of sin. No part of our world has been left untouched. As Paul declares in his letter to the Romans, "For we know that the whole creation has been groaning together in the pains of childbirth until now" (Rom 8:22).

Despite the effects of sin, the goodness of creation remains. It does not stop being good because of sin. To see this, it may be helpful to make a distinction between the *structure* of creation and the *direction* of creation (we'll consider this more fully in chapter 10). When theologians speak of the structure of creation, they mean that God created the world with a certain shape and order to it. The structure of an entity is that which makes it what it is. It is what philosophers in the West call a "nature," "substance," or "essence." Direction, on the other hand, refers to how something is moved or used. If, as the Christian metanarrative recognizes, this distinction between structure and direction is correct, every decision we make and every action we take is theological in nature. Every aspect of our worldview should be directed and shaped by our theology.[16]

In this section we've established the principle that everything is essentially theological. Let us now consider another theological principle that builds on and flows out of this first principle—*all truth is God's truth.*

All Truth Is God's Truth

Since their formation in the West, universities have held up theology as the queen of the sciences. But from the Enlightenment on, theology has fallen on hard times. No longer is theology a required area of study for secular institutions of higher learning, even among those once founded on Christian principles; it is reserved for divinity or religious studies majors. Even then, such circles are inundated with religious pluralism, relativism, and various other non-Christian worldviews and ideologies.

---

[15]For a helpful resource, see *Albert M. Wolters, Creation Regained: Biblical Basics for a Reformational Worldview*, 2nd ed. (Grand Rapids, MI: Wm. B. Eerdmans Publishing Company, 2005).

[16]Ibid., 59.

In contrast to many secular schools, students at Christian colleges and universities are at a distinct advantage. Like most secular universities, Christian colleges and universities offer a wide range of disciplines. Students attending Christian schools are interested in being lawyers, doctors, surgeons, engineers, and journalists; yet, for most Christian centers of higher education, introductory theology and biblical studies courses are required for all students to take. What the ancients understood in establishing theology as the queen of the sciences, and what many Christ-centered Christian universities and colleges understand today, is that theology serves as the key integrating point for all other disciplines. Along with the early church, the establishers of the university recognized that God, as the all-wise and good Creator of all things, is also the source and ground of all knowledge, wisdom, and truth (Prv 2:6; Dan 2:20; Rom 11:33, 36; 1 Cor 2:7; Col 2:2-3). As Arthur Holmes so eloquently put it:

> The early church claimed that all truth is God's truth wherever it be found. The *focus* here is on truth. But the ultimate *locus* of truth is God. If he is the eternal and all-wise creator of all things, as Christians affirm, then his creative wisdom is the source and norm of all truth about everything. And if God and his wisdom are unchangingly the same, then truth is likewise unchanging and thus *universal*. If all truth is his, and he understands fully its interrelatedness, then truth is *unified* in his perfect understanding.[17]

The world in which we live is rational and understandable because God, as the source and ground of all knowledge and truth, is Himself rational. Moreover, human beings, who are made in the image and likeness of God, are created in such a way that they can know and understand their Creator and the world in which He has made. Our *noetic structures*[18] and *cognitive faculties*[19] are geared toward finding truth.

Recognizing that all truth is God's truth doesn't mean that truth is found only in the Bible, as some have argued. Historically, Christianity has recognized two books of revelation—the Book of God's Word (special or supernatural revelation) and the Book of Nature (general or natural revelation). The book of God's Word provides us with knowledge about God and His workings in the world that we could not have known through human reasoning and observation alone. Theologically speaking, revelation is a disclosure or unveiling of some knowledge. As special revelation, the Bible is God's self-disclosure of Himself to His human creatures that could not have been garnered from nature. Through it, we learn of God's tri-unity and His work in reconciling the world to Himself through the culmination of salvation history.

---

[17]Arthur F. Holmes, *All Truth is Gods Truth* (Downers Grove, IL: InterVarsity Press, 1977), 8.

[18]A "noetic structure" refers to the total range of beliefs that any given individual may have. For a good discussion, see Ronald H. Nash, *Faith and Reason: Searching for a Rational Faith* (Grand Rapids, MI: Zondervan, 1988), 21-24.

[19]Cognitive faculties are those mental capacities that enable us to understand, process, reason, and make sense of the various phenomena of our world.

God's Word is authoritative for all of life and truthful (inerrant) in all that it affirms; however, we must be clear that it is not exhaustive in what it tells us about the world. In other words, the Bible *speaks to* (authority) all things, but there are some things that the Bible does not *speak on* (knowledge). For example, the Bible says nothing *about* (speaking on) Cantor's Theorem or quantum physics. Though the Bible doesn't *speak on* every topic we'll ever encounter, it does provide a framework by which we can approach our understanding and evaluate each of these subjects as Christians. Throughout God's Word, He has given us commands and biblical principles that guide us in our decisions and that help us in understanding His good world. [20] As people of the word, *we seek to understand God's good world through the lens of God's special revelation.* Understanding that all truth is God's truth, whether found in the Book of Nature or in the Book of God's Word, brings coherence to knowledge and truth.

Before ending this chapter, it would be profitable to take some space to discuss the nature of truth. There are three contenders for a viable theory of truth: the correspondence theory, the coherentist theory, and the pragmatic theory. We'll briefly consider each and then assess whether one theory best fits with the biblical understanding of truth.

The correspondence theory has been the predominate theory up until the nineteenth century, so, we'll begin with it. The correspondence theory suggests that propositions (statements, beliefs, and thoughts) correspond to reality. In other words, truth obtains when a proposition properly represents or reflects reality as it is. Take the proposition, "it is raining outside my window." If I look outside my window and it's raining, then the proposition "it is raining outside my window" is true. If instead I look outside my window and it's bright and sunny with no rain, then the proposition "it is raining outside my widow" is false. The coherence theory of truth, in contrast, suggests that a belief or proposition is true only so far as it coheres with the entirety of one's set of beliefs. Lastly, the pragmatic theory, most prominently advocated by William James (1842-1910), suggests that a proposition is true so long as that proposition *works* or *is useful for one to have.*[21] Let's consider some of the difficulties that coherentist and pragmatic theories face, and then we'll turn to the biblical view on truth.

One of the key problems with the coherence theory is that the central test of truth is whether or not one's belief coheres with all other things that one knows. But often, stories, such as fairytales, are logically consistent, and yet one wouldn't believe that such stories are true simply because they are logically consistent or

---

[20]We will discuss this more in depth in the final chapter on integration. For a helpful resource on integrating biblical principles into one's discipline and subject, see Mark Eckel, *The Whole Truth: Classroom Strategies for Biblical Integration* (Chicago, IL: Xulon Press, 2003). See also, Arthur F. Holmes, *Contours of a World View* (Grand Rapids, MI: William B. Eerdmans Publishing, 1983); W. David Beck, ed., *Opening the American Mind: The Integration of Biblical Truth in the Curriculum of the University* (Grand Rapids, MI: Baker Publishing Group, 1991).

[21]J. P. Moreland and William Lane Craig, *Philosophical Foundations for a Christian Worldview* (Downers Grove, IL: InterVarsity Press, 2003), 131-144.

coherent. At other times, people make up lies that seem to be logically consistent, but don't, in the end, match up with reality. Perhaps, most damaging to the coherence theory is that it violates an important law of logic—the law of non-contradiction. Simply put, the law of non-contradiction states that something cannot be both true and false at the same time and in the same sense. [22] Let's return to our example of whether it is raining outside my window or not. Given the law of non-contradiction, either it is raining outside my window or it isn't. But someone might retort: "there have been times when driving I've observed that it was raining in one spot and not in another. In that case, it was raining outside and it wasn't raining outside. There's no contradiction." But that's not exactly what we're saying, here. Perhaps, some clarification is in order. What we mean is that it cannot be both raining outside my window and not raining outside my window in the same spot, at the same time, and in the same manner. To claim that it is both raining outside and not raining outside, *in a particular spot, at the same time, and in the same manner* would be a contradiction. So, how does this play out in the coherentist's understanding of truth? Since truth for the coherentist has to do with whether or not the thing being believed coheres with all other things that one knows, then it is conceivable that a person can have contradictory beliefs, so long as those beliefs coherently fit together into the totality of her beliefs. But because of the law of non-contradiction, two contradictory claims cannot both be true.

What of the pragmatic theory? In some ways, it's more radical than the coherentist view; yet it has equally as many difficulties. Like the coherentist's perspective on truth, something that is considered to be "true" may not line up with how things are in reality. Moreover, for the pragmatic view, truth becomes whatever one wants it to be, so long as it "works" for the person or group. In other words, truth becomes relative. What's so bad about relativism? There are several difficulties with relativism, but I'll consider two. First, relativism is self-contradictory, or as philosophers often say, "self-refuting" or "self-referentially incoherent." Relativists believe that truth is relative and that there are no absolute truths, that is to say, truths that apply to all people in all circumstances. The problem, however, is that relativists believe that relativism applies to all people. In other words, relativists make an absolute claim, namely, *that all truth is relative.* But if that's the case, then relativism is contradictory and self-refuting. It breaks the law of non-contradiction. A second difficulty is that relativists often base their view of relativism on the belief that people have differing viewpoints. But this is ultimately paradoxical, since the defender of objective truth can discern two truths from this: (1) it is true (not false) that people have varying viewpoints and (2) it is true (not false) that one can conclude relativism based on the belief that there are varying viewpoints. Relativism ultimately fails.[23]

---

[22]Chad V. Meister, *Building Belief: Constructing Faith from the Ground Up* (Grand Rapids, MI: Baker Books, 2006), 21-28.

[23]Paul Copan, *That's Just Your Interpretation: Responding to Skeptics Who Challenge Your Faith* (Grand Rapids, MI: Baker books, 2001), 26-27.

Unlike coherentist and pragmatist theories, the correspondence theory of truth carries with it a deep connection to reality. Moreover, it doesn't fall into relativism, nor does it break the law of non-contradiction. But is it the biblical view of truth?

Unfortunately, the Bible doesn't spell out one particular theory on truth, but thankfully it does have quite a bit to say about the nature of truth. William Lane Craig and J.P. Moreland sum up the biblical understanding of truth in the following way: "The Old and New Testament terms for truth are, respectively *'emet* and *alētheia.* The meaning of these terms and, more generally, a biblical conception of truth are broad and multifaceted: fidelity, moral rectitude, being real, being genuine, faithfulness, having veracity, being complete." [24] As Craig and Moreland suggest here, the biblical understanding of truth is not one-dimensional; rather, it is multi-dimensional. Truth doesn't have to do merely with the abstract or propositions, as some suppose, but carries over into the sphere of personal and moral life. They continue:

> Two aspects of the biblical conception of truth appear to be primary: faithfulness and conformity to fact. The latter appears to presuppose a correspondence theory. Arguably, the former appears to involve a correspondence theory. Thus faithfulness may be understood as a person's actions' corresponding to the person's assertions or promises, and a similar point could be made about genuineness, moral rectitude and so forth. [25]

As Craig and Moreland further point out, this multi-dimensional view of truth, then, may quite well fit with the correspondence theory. So, in our assessment, the correspondence theory best explains the nature of truth and best fits with the biblical description of truth.

So, what might we take away from our discussion on truth? Let's summarize:

- Truth is best understood as beliefs or propositions that correspond with reality (i.e., the way things are)—the correspondence theory

- Truth is objective, not relative

- Truth, in the biblical perspective, is multi-dimensional and multifaceted.

- Truth has to do not merely with the abstract thinking, but also with the personal and moral spheres of our lives

Ultimately, all truth is God's truth since God is the rational Creator of all things. All wisdom and knowledge are grounded in Him. As the Apostle Paul wrote long ago in his letter to the Romans:

> [33] Oh, the depth of the riches and wisdom and knowledge of God! How unsearchable are his judgments and how inscrutable his ways!

---

[24] Craig and Moreland, *Philosophical Foundations,* 131.
[25] Ibid.

[34] "For who has known the mind of the Lord,

or who has been his counselor?"

[35] "Or who has given a gift to him

that he might be repaid?"

[36] For from him and through him and to him are all things. To him be glory forever. Amen. (Rom 11:33-36)

Conclusion

In this chapter, I've begun to build a case for why studying theology is important. Hopefully, you're beginning to see its relevance, too. In the remaining chapters, we're going to look at nine more reasons why theology is vital for living out the Christian life. As we conclude, I want to leave you with this charge. Let us buck the system of complacency and anti-intellectualism and reclaim our minds for Christ. Let us begin to submerge ourselves into the depths of *theology*.

Chapter Two

Shaping a Worldview

Thinking Outside the Box

The word "worldview" has become somewhat cliché in Christian culture, but it is, nevertheless, an important concept to think about. So, why should anyone concern themselves with studying the concept of worldview, especially when reading a book on theology? The obvious reason is that everyone has one, even if a person is unaware of it. Everyone forms a variety of beliefs about the most important issues in life. These beliefs in turn inform how a person lives, makes decisions, and reacts to situations in the world. Studying worldview provides a clearer picture of the world and makes available an overarching coherence to all of life. As Albert Wolters notes, a worldview functions as a sort of life guide or road map, helping a person to make important decisions about various issues in life.[1]

Who should I vote for in the up-coming election? Should I take a job that will require more hours away from my family? Can a person be a Christian and yet be an actor? Is it wrong to have an abortion? How do I choose a career? Worldviews are the kinds of things that people simply cannot live without, despite their awareness or lack of awareness of them.

Forming a consistent and coherent worldview not only helps us answer the pressing questions of life, but such a task also helps us to wrestle with the ultimate questions about life. "Who is God?" "What is real?" "What can we know?" "Why is there anything at all?" "Is there any purpose and meaning to this life?" "Do moral absolutes exist?" Every worldview captures six major categories of questions:

> ***God***: Does God exist? If so, what kind of God exists? What is God like? Is there more than one god? What is God's relationship to the world?

> ***Ultimate Reality***: Is the universe all there is? How did the universe come about? Did God create the universe, or is the universe (at least the basic building blocks) eternal? Does God need the world for His existence or does God exist apart from

---

[1]Albert M. Wolters, *Creation Regained: Biblical Basics for a Reformational Worldview*, second edition (Grand Rapids, MI: Wm. B. Eerdmans Publishing Co., 2005), 5.

the universe? Does reality consist of only material objects, or does it also contain an immaterial dimension to it.

Humanity: How did humans arrive on the earth? Were humans created or were they the result of evolutionary processes? Are humans ultimately material creatures, or do they consist of both a material and immaterial part? What separates humans from other animal species?

Knowledge: What can I know? Is knowledge about the external world possible? Can God be known? Is belief in God rational? What is the relation between faith and reason? What is truth? Do absolute truths exists, or is all truth relative? Is the past knowable?

Ethics: How should I live? Who determines right from wrong? Do objective moral standards exist, or all moral decisions based on the individual or society?

Afterlife: What happens after I die? Is there a place beyond the world, or is life in this world it? Will I get to see loved ones again? Does a person experience reincarnation?[2]

These six categories overlap with the major categories and themes often found in philosophical and theological discourse. While the average person has not developed a fully functioning theological or philosophical system, most have given some thought to the questions above.

Not only do these six categories overlap with theology and philosophy, but our beliefs concerning these categories are interconnected, forming, as discussed in the previous chapter, a "web" of beliefs. Within this web or system, some beliefs are more central than others, which we've been calling "control beliefs." As we'll see below, our theological beliefs shape our worldviews significantly, especially our beliefs about God and the God-world relationship. What people believe about God influences or directs many of their other beliefs. For now, let's consider some reasons why Christians ought to study and think hard about their own worldview and the worldviews of others.

For Christians, understanding one's worldview is essential for several reasons. One such reason is missions and evangelism. In Matthew 28:19-20, Jesus charges His disciples with the task to "go therefore and make disciples of all nations." But making disciples is not always an easy task. Not only do cultural and linguistic barriers exist, but ideological barriers stand in the way, as well. When encounter-

---

[2]For additional ways to categorize worldviews see the following: Ronald Nash, *Worldviews in Conflict: Choosing Christianity in a World of Ideas* (Grand Rapids, MI: Zondervan, 1992); James W. Sire, *The Universe Next Door*, 5th ed. (Downers Grove, IL: InterVarsity Press, 2009); Mark P. Cosgrove, *Foundations of Christian Thought: Faith, Learning, and the Christian Worldview* (Grand Rapids, MI: Kregel, 2006); Norman L. Geisler and William D. Watkins, *Perspectives: Understanding and Evaluating Today's World Views* (San Bernardino: Here's Life Publishers, 1984; Chad V. Meister, *Building Belief: Constructing Faith from the Ground Up* (Grand Rapids, MI: Baker Books, 2006).

ing people from different faiths or cultures, it is important to consider that they often don't think the way we do, nor do they have the same terminology or cultural norms. Certain conceptions of reality and of God may cause two interlocutors to speak past one another. But we need not go outside of our immediate surroundings or cultural context to find those who have opposing worldviews. Differing worldviews are all around thanks to media, technology, and globalization.[3] Thus understanding the basic structures that lie behind, not only one's own worldview, but also how others think and act, will promote richer and more fruitful dialogue between people of differing worldviews and faiths.

Closely tied to evangelism and mission work is the task of Christian apologetics. Apologetics is the discipline of theology that seeks to give a rational defense of the Christian faith. (I will consider the task of apologetics more fully in the next chapter, but, for now, it is enough to note that non-religious folk and people of other faiths often ask Christians to give reasons for their beliefs.) Often, a Christian may need to engage in apologetics before evangelizing. It may be necessary to remove some of the intellectual barriers and obstacles that a person has before being open to hearing the message of the gospel. On the flip side, apologetics not only serves as a means for defending Christianity and providing answers to unbelievers, it also serves in bolstering a believer's faith. By comparing the differences between various worldviews, Christians can see how their own worldview measures up to that of others. Understanding various worldviews can be a powerful tool to the apologist.

Another reason Christians should think hard about the concept of worldview is personal enrichment. Why personal enrichment? God created the world for our enjoyment (Gen 1:3, 10, 11, 18, 21, 25, 28-31; 2:8-9). In addition, as God's image bearers, we were created in a unique way—"a little lower than the heavenly beings" (Ps 8:5). Again, as we saw in the previous chapter, God has given humans the ability to understand the world. No other earthly creature has the ability to understand, explore, and grow in knowledge of the created world. In the book of Colossians, we are told that it is in Christ that all wisdom and knowledge dwells (Col 2:2-3). Moreover, it was Christ who created all things and sustains the world in existence (Jn 1:3; Col 1:16-17; Heb 1:2-3). From the Christian perspective, God created the world rationally, that is, the world is knowable. Because we are His image-bearers, like God—but in a limited way—we can know the world. Our limits in understanding the world are, in part, a result of our finite nature, but, also, in part, because of the effects of sin on our cognitive faculties. Sin has distorted our abilities to view and understand the world. Nevertheless, sin has not erased our capacity for understanding, exploring, and enjoying the good world which God created and in which we live.

---

[3]Globalization is a difficult term, one that is easier to recognize than to define. Roughly, globalization refers to the widespread perception of the increasing speed and advancement of the interconnectedness of all spheres of life (economic, cultural, political, and religious), much of which has been brought about by advancements in technology.

As noted above, sin has distorted the human understanding of the world. We were created to enjoy God, to enjoy one another, and to enjoy the good world that God created, but in order to do this fully, humans are in need of redemption. Part of the reason that we study is to gain a clearer understanding of the human condition, and to learn ways in which we can strive to become how God originally intended us to be, in the world that God intended us to live in. Yet, this can only come about through God's redemptive work. God is restoring the world (Col 1:20) and we are to be used by God as agents for change (2 Cor 5:17-21). Yet, to do this, not only must we learn to conform in behavior, we must also come to recognize false ideologies.

Some Christians may object to worldview study because they see such an exercise as being too intellectual. After all, isn't the Christian life about simple faith? To add all this talk of worldview is nothing more than to bog down the gospel with unnecessary speculation. How might we respond to this objection? The Bible surely tells us that we are to come to faith in Jesus much like a child (Mk 10:13). Yet, having a childlike faith doesn't mean neglecting the formation of the mind. As J. P. Moreland rightly points out, study is a spiritual discipline.[4] Further, Scripture speaks often of the importance of the formation of the mind. As we saw in the last chapter, Christians are to love God with all their "minds," and are to give every aspect of who they are over to the lordship of Christ—including their thoughts, beliefs, behaviors, traditions, and disciplines. If some belief, idea, or behavior opposes Christ and His kingdom, then it should be abandoned.

Yet, there is another reason why Christians ought to study worldview—to watch for false teachers. Jesus warned believers to watch out for false prophets who come in "sheep's clothing," but who inwardly are "ferocious wolves" (Matt 7:15, NIV). Believers are to recognize these false teachers by their "fruits," or in other words, by what they say (7:16-20). In the pastoral epistles, the apostle Paul warns his young apprentice, Timothy, against allowing false teachers into the church (1 Tim 4:1-2; 2 Tim 2:16-18; 3:13; 4:3-4). We see the same warnings given in the books of Jude and 2 Peter (2:1-22). Ultimately, as followers of Jesus, we are to know what we believe and why we believe it, and we are to defend such beliefs against false teaching.

As this book unfolds, we're going to consider many of these reasons in greater detail, especially as they relate to theology. But for now, let's take some space to define just what a worldview is.

Gazing into the Mind's Eye

Throughout the first part of this chapter we hinted at elements that make up a worldview, but we did not nail down a specific definition. Before we do that, it's important to consider what a worldview is not.

---

[4]J. P. Moreland, "Philosophy," in *Opening the American Mind: The Integration of Biblical Truth in the Curriculum of the University*, ed. W. David Beck (Grand Rapids, MI: Baker Book House, 1991), 53.

As noted above, a worldview *is not* a certain theology or philosophy, yet, it includes many overlapping themes and elements found in both theological and philosophical investigation. Not only that, our theological and philosophical beliefs shape our worldviews. As discussed in chapter one, theology is that discipline which seeks to understand who God is, what God is like, and what God's relationship to the world involves. In coming to grips with the God-world relationship, a person also learns what it means to be human, and especially a human in relation to God, other humans, and the rest of the created space-time universe. Philosophy, on the other hand, does not presume whether God exists, what humans are like, or whether the space-time universe has always existed. Philosophy is, what J. P. Moreland calls, a second-order discipline, that is, it's a discipline that studies other disciplines.[5] Philosophy is a powerful tool that helps a person to analyze certain views on the nature of reality and how we can know it. How does worldview study differ from these two disciplines? There are at least two ways. First, not all worldviews adhere to a certain theology or source for theological inquiry (e.g., Bible, Koran, or Talmud). That doesn't mean, however, that such worldviews lack theological convictions. Atheism, for example, is the view that no god or gods exists. While the worldview of atheism does not adhere to any one theology, it does, nevertheless, make a theological claim—namely, that no god or gods exist.[6] Second, if we are to understand philosophy as a second-order discipline, then it would be appropriate to say that no one such worldview is a philosophy, but rather, people utilize philosophy in developing their worldviews.

Having considered what a worldview is not, we turn to what it is. The English word "worldview" comes from the German word *Weltanschauung* and was first coined by Immanuel Kant.[7] To put it quite simply, a worldview is, in the words of Ronald Nash, "a set of beliefs about the most important issues in life."[8] Nash's definition of a worldview is helpful but needs some clarification and explication. For our purposes in this chapter and book, worldviews are *interpretive grids, consisting of a variety of beliefs and attitudes, by which people filter through the data from the world, allowing them to form a consistent and coherent view of reality, in order to make sense of all of life.* That's quite a mouthful. Let's take a moment to unpack each major point.

First, let's consider the notion of "interpretive grids . . . by which people filter through the data from the world." Every person interprets reality, but not everyone's interpretation is the same. Each of us has a certain *structure* or *framework* we bring to the world to make sense of it. We might think of an interpretive grid as a multi-layered filter that helps us develop our beliefs about the world. Within

---

[5]Ibid., 49.

[6]Not only is this a theological claim, but it is also a metaphysical claim. Metaphysics is a branch of philosophical investigation that deals with claims about the nature of reality.

[7]Paul G. Hiebert, *Transforming Worldviews: An Anthropological Understanding of How People Change* (Grand Rapids, MI: Baker Academic, 2008), 13; David K. Naugle, *Worldview: The History of a Concept* (Grand Rapids, MI: William B. Eerdmans Publishing Co., 2002), 58.

[8]Ronald Nash, *Worldviews*, 16.

any given interpretive grid, there are philosophical and theological factors, as well as scientific, psychological, sociological, and historical factors, all of which contribute to an individual's overall set of beliefs about the world. When faced with data from the world, people either accept or reject the data depending upon those beliefs in the interpretive grid that are most basic and foundational to their *noetic structure*, and to which they're most committed—what we've been calling *control beliefs*.[9] For example, a person may hold to a certain theological conviction that God created human beings in His image and likeness, which in turn may inform for that person the outcome of certain socio-cultural beliefs about how humans are to be treated within society. Another way to think of an interpretive grid may be analogous to viewing the world through colored glasses.[10] If one wears glasses with yellow lenses, then the world looks yellow. In a similar manner, if one adheres to Islam, then one deciphers the data of the world through the interpretive lens (grid) of Islam. However, there are certain limitations to such an analogy. As noted by philosopher J.P. Moreland, "Glasses stand between a person and the external world such that a person's access to reality is mediated *through* the glasses."[11] We must avoid any notion that something stands between a person directly knowing and experiencing reality, since persons are *capable of* and *do* change their beliefs. "A better way to describe the role of a worldview in seeing reality," says Moreland, "is to depict it as a habituated way of directing our attention or inattention, as the case may be."[12] Moreland's emphasis on habits helps to accentuate the person's capacity to change beliefs, including one's control beliefs, even if the person is not accustomed to doing so. A person, with enough effort, can see other perspectives and consider contrary evidence or facts.

The second element is "consisting of a variety of beliefs and attitudes." Beliefs are propositional in nature, and they vary among people, ranging from *foundational* beliefs, such as the belief that God exists, and *less foundational beliefs*, such as I had oatmeal for breakfast this morning. Foundational beliefs, or *presuppositions*, make up the core of a person's worldview. Concerning presuppositions, Ronald Nash has this to say: "We all hold a number of beliefs that we presuppose or accept without support from other beliefs or arguments or evidence. Such presuppositions are necessary if we are to think at all. . . . we must believe something before we can know anything."[13] Presuppositions are the most basic beliefs about life—beliefs about God, human beings, and the world—which direct people toward a certain outlook on life and toward a certain way of living. For example, based on their presuppositions, Christians come to an entirely different set of conclusions about the afterlife than do, say, Buddhists or atheists. Fur-

---

[9]David K. Clark, *Dialogical Apologetics: A Person-Centered Approach to Christian Defense* (Grand Rapids, MI: Baker, 1993), 77.

[10]Geisler and Watkins, *Perspectives*, 11.

[11]J. P. Moreland, *The Kingdom Triangle: Recover the Christian Mind, Renovate the Soul, Restore the Spirit's Power* (Grand Rapids, MI: Zondervan, 2007), 33.

[12]Ibid.

[13]Nash, *Worldviews*, 21.

thermore, presuppositions, as James Sire points out, can be either "conscious" or "subconscious," "true or false," "consistent or inconsistent."[14] On the other hand, less foundational beliefs, or "suppositions," [15] as Thomas Morris calls them, are the kinds of beliefs that are constantly changing, and are often formed from our presuppositions. These beliefs do not make up the core of one's worldview. For individuals to change their suppositions, it would not deeply affect their overall worldview. Yet, as Morris rightly points out, presuppositions and suppositions are not the only factors that contribute to a person's outlook on life. People also have "predispositions" and "dispositions."[16] Predispositions are "non-propositional" and refer to a person's basic character traits or "personality orientation."[17] Dispositions, on the other hand, are those attitudes and moods that are "more changeable"[18] on a day-to-day basis. In other words, how we feel, whether temporary or long-term, often affects our acceptance or rejection of certain beliefs.

Third, the statements "to form a consistent and coherent view of reality" and "to make sense of all of life" refer to the testability of a person's worldview.[19] Whether people realize it or not, they strive for having a consistent and coherent worldview. They need to make sense of life, and they often have a preconceived understanding of what the "good life" consists of. Obviously, though, not everyone uses the same criteria for testing worldviews. Some people have no (conscious) criteria. Others hold *a priori* certain criteria, while rejecting others.

Given that more than one worldview exists, how might individuals discern between conflicting ways of viewing and understanding the world? Much like any scientific theory, a person's worldview is testable. While not exhaustive, there are four common tests to use when evaluating worldview claims: 1) the test of logical consistency; 2) the test of experience; 3) the test of explanatory power; and 4) the test of livability.

Logical consistency: First, we must ask whether our worldviews are logically consistent. Logic is extremely important for everyday living and for making sense of the world. People use logic all the time, often without realizing it. The fundamental law of logic is the law of non-contradiction. As discussed in chapter one, the Law of non-contradiction states that some item *A* cannot be both *B* and *non-B* in the same sense and at the same time. For instance, Plato cannot be both a human and non-human at the same time. If he is human, then he cannot be other than human. To say that Plato is both human and extra-terrestrial would be a contradiction. But as William Hasker rightly points out, not all inconsisten-

---

[14]James W. Sire, *Naming the Elephant* (Downers Grove, IL: InterVarsity Press, 2004), 130

[15]Thomas Morris, *Francis Schaeffer's Apologetic: A Critique* (Chicago: Moody Press, 1976), 109.

[16]Ibid., 113.

[17]Ibid.

[18]Ibid., 114.

[19]William Hasker, *Metaphysics: Constructing a World View* (Downers Grove, IL: InterVarsity Press, 1983), 25-28 .

cies are as noticeable as the above example.[20] Often, inconsistencies are subtle and can be difficult to recognize. One reason for this is that many people practice *syncretism*—the acceptance of beliefs that are contradictory to one's worldview—without even realizing it.

Experience: Not only should a person's worldview be logically consistent, but such a worldview should coincide with one's experiences of the world. Our worldviews should correlate with the facts we perceive in the world. As Ronald Nash insightfully says, "We have a right to expect world-views to touch base with human experience. World-views should throw light on our experiences of the world. They should explain our experiences easily and naturally, and they should be relevant to what we know about the world and ourselves."[21] This doesn't mean, however, that humans are infallible when they interpret empirical data and experience. Lastly, human experience should not be the only test for a person's worldview.

Explanatory Power: It's not enough that a person's worldview is logically consistent, nor is it enough for a person to have all the facts. Worldviews must also provide explanatory power. Concerning this criterion, Hasker writes:

> Suppose, for example, a physicist has been conducting a series of experiments on radioactive decay and has compiled an exhaustive set of records giving the conditions and results of each experiment. When we ask him to explain his results, he simply hands over his records of the experiments. Clearly, he hasn't done what we asked of him, but why not? His records, we may assume, contain no logical inconsistencies, and they fit the facts as well as anyone could desire—better, in fact, than any theory that could be provided. . . . But however admirable in both of these respects, the scientist's records are totally lacking in explanatory power. They do nothing, that is, to unify the experimental data with each other or with other knowledge in the field; the give us nothing of the causes of the observed phenomena; they give us no hint of the causes of the observed phenomena; they give us no sense whatever that we have comprehended what is going on. The feeling of insight, of enlightenment, that is the subjective accompaniment of understanding, is entirely lacking.[22]

In addition, Hasker suggests that a good theory provides us with unity, a cause, and comprehensiveness.[23]

Livability: There is one last criterion to consider—the criterion of livability. This test asks: "Is my worldview livable?" The test of livability is not one too often considered, but is nevertheless an important one. As Francis Schaefer reminds us, "every person has the pull of two consistencies, the pull towards the real world and the pull towards the logic of his system."[24] What good is a worldview if, after

[20]Ibid., 27.

[21]Nash, Ronald H. Nash, *Faith and Reason: Searching for a Rational Faith* (Grand Rapids, MI: Zondervan, 1988), 55.

[22]Hasker, *Metaphysics*, p. 27.

[23]Ibid.

[24]Francis Schaefer, *The God Who Is There*, 2nd ed. (Downers Grove, IL: InterVarsity Press, 1982), 152

having shown that it is logically consistent with one's presuppositions, coheres with experience and empirical data, and provides explanatory power, but is impossible to live it out in a consistent manner?

Therefore, any worldview should be logically consistent, fit the relevant facts, provide the proper explanatory power to make sense of the world, and be livable. When all four criterions have properly been considered and each test has been met, one's worldview provides the *best explanation*.

What Hath Theology to Do with a Worldview?

Now on to wrapping up a matter discussed earlier, one of which needs further explication. There are many worldviews that do not practice the discipline of theology, yet, it would be inaccurate to think that those worldviews have nothing theological to say. As noted above, even worldviews or religions which deny the existence of a god or gods (e.g., atheism or Buddhism) do, nevertheless, make theological judgments.

When trying to come to grips with one's worldview, perhaps the most fundamental question is if God exists. Here we must ask: "What kind of God exists, if at all?" "What is God's relationship to the world?" "Can humans even know that such a God exists?" "If God exists, what should be our response to Him?" If God exists, then such questions are pressing and bear strongly on the various other aspects of one's worldview. It could be argued that what one does with God strongly influences or directs all other aspects of one's worldview. Thus, all other parts of a worldview boil down to a theological question.

There are three broad worldviews, each of which provide a different perspective on ultimate reality and the God/world relationship, and which most philosophers and theologians consider to be 'live options' among alternatives today: theism, naturalism, and pantheism.[25] Let's consider each of these in turn, beginning with theism.

Theism is the belief that exactly one God exists, a view held by each of the three major monotheistic religions (Christianity, Islam, and Judaism), as well as some varieties of Hinduism and African religions. The God of theism is non-physical (spirit) in nature, personal, morally perfect, omnipotent (all-powerful), omniscient (all-knowing), eternal, and the creator of all things. When theists speak

---

[25]There are other worldviews that could have been included in our discussion, such as deism, finite godism, or panentheism. In some ways, deism and finite godhism are similar to theism, but they differ in significant ways. Deism is the view that God created the world, but transcends the created order. The God of deism is either non-personal or He chooses not to personally interact with the world. Adherents of finite godhism generally deny one of God's essential or core attributes, such as divine omnipotence or that God is essentially loving. Panentheists, on the other hand, identify with pantheists in claiming that the world in some sense exists "in" God; yet, like theists, God transcends the world. A popular example that panentheists give is that of the soul's relation to the body. God is the soul of the world. Just as the soul transcends the body, but is, nevertheless, intricately connected to it, the same is true of God's relationship to the world.

of God as Creator, they mean that the eternal God created the four-dimensional space-time universe out of nothing (*ex nihilo*), that is, out of no pre-existing matter or things. Furthermore, to make the theistic view of creation more radical, heaven itself is not an eternal place; rather, it, too, is a creation of God. Prior to God's creative working, He alone existed. God alone is eternal and uncreated. Furthermore, unlike the god of pantheism (which we'll see below), the God of theism is personal and morally perfect. By "personal," theists mean that God cares for and is concerned for His creatures. He engages with them in a variety of ways. By "morally perfect," theists mean that God neither does any evil, nor could He ever do anything that is evil. His character is such that God always does that which is good and just.

Naturalists, on the other hand, believe that the universe is all there is. It would be helpful to note, before explaining the naturalistic view of God/Ultimate Reality, that there are a variety of naturalists in the world. Like theists, they do not fit into one specific mold. There are, on the one hand, *methodological* naturalists, and, on the other, *metaphysical* naturalists. Methodological naturalists seek to approach the world as if there is no supernatural. They may, in fact, believe that a god or gods exist; yet, they choose to approach their understanding of the world scientifically and as if no god or gods exist. Generally, they take their belief in God apart from the need for any kind of evidence—such a view is known as *fideism*. While methodological naturalists allow room for the existence of a god or gods, metaphysical naturalists do not. With respect to reality, what one sees is what one gets. All that exists is the natural processes that make up the four-dimensional space-time universe in which we live. Some allow for the possibility that there are many universes in addition to our own. But ultimately there is nothing beyond nature. Matter is eternal and has always existed, in some sense or another. The universe is a closed system of cause and effect, and, therefore, there is no room for outside engagement from something beyond the universe—no miracles. Some people confuse atheists and agnostics with naturalists. But it's important to keep in mind that not all atheists and agnostics are naturalists. Naturalism is a stronger position than either atheism or agnosticism. After all, some atheists, though they don't believe in a divine entity, nevertheless embraces certain philosophical systems like Platonism. Furthermore, some agnostics believe that a divine being may very well exist; however, we can't know what this being is like. Despite this, there are a good number of atheists and agnostics who do lean toward a naturalistic understanding of what is ultimately real.

The third live option is pantheism. In some ways, pantheism is distinct from theism and naturalism, yet it shares similarities with each view. Like theism, pantheists accept that some kind of god exists. This god is not personal, like the god of theism (hence the lowercase "g" when speaking of god); rather, god is more like a unifying force that runs through all of existence. Moreover, the pantheistic god doesn't transcend creation, but is entirely immanent, that is, god is identical to the world. Hence the prefix "pan," which means "all." God is all and all is god. There is no differentiation. Yet, like naturalists, most pantheists (though, not all) reject the idea that reality is made up of more than one substance or thing—a view known as *monism.* Some pantheists are also polytheists or henotheists. *Polytheism* is the view that more than one god exists, much like one finds in the ancient Roman, Greek, and Nordic pantheon of gods. Similarly to polytheism, *henotheism* holds to the view that more than one god exists, yet it differs in recognizing that a local deity or one deity reigns supreme over the others. *The Bhagavad Gita* provides a helpful glimpse of the Hindu pantheistic conception of god. In the following passage, the Hindu god, Krishna, who, in the *Gita*, is the incarnation of Brahman, allows the ancient warrior Arjuna to capture a glimpse of "the supreme mystery of the Self."[26] Arjuna responds by saying,

> 15   O Lord, I see within your body all the gods and every kind of living creatures. I see Brahma, the Creator, seated on a lotus; I see the ancient sages and the celestial serpents.
>
> 16   I see infinite mouths and arms, stomach and eyes, and you are embodied in every form. I see you everywhere, without beginning, middle, or end. You are Lord of all creation, and the cosmos is your body.
>
> 17   You wear a crown and carry a mace and discus; your radiance is blinding and immeasurable. I see you, who are so difficult to behold, shining like a fiery sun blazing in every direction.
>
> 18   You are supreme, changeless Reality, the one thing to be known. You are the refuge of all creation, the immortal spirit, the eternal guardian of eternal dharma.
>
> 19   You are without beginning, middle, or end; you touch everything with your infinite power. The sun and moon are your eyes, and your mouth is fire; your radiance warms the cosmos.
>
> 20   O Lord, your presence fills the heavens and the earth and reaches in every direction. I see the three worlds trembling before this vision of your wonderful and terrible form.[27]

From this passage, it becomes clear how everything, even the gods, in some sense or another, is one with Brahma.

Christians are theists. Like all other theists, they believe that God created the universe *ex nihilo* (Gen 1; Jn 1:1-3; 1 Cor 8:6; Col 1:16; Heb 1:2). As the Creator of all things, all things belong to Him (Ps 24:1-2) and stand under His Lordship. Moral agents who were created in God's image and likeness (Gen 1:26-27; 9:6; Js 3:9), and who belong to Him, are responsible to Him (Gen 2:16-17; Rom 2:6; 1 Cor 3:10-15; 2 Cor 5:10; Rev 20:12-15). There is, however, one key distinction (though, no doubt others exist) between the Christian God and the god of other theists, namely, God is a tri-unity of persons—Father, Son, and Holy Spirit. There are not three distinct or separate gods (tritheism), nor is there one god who morphs from the Father, to the Son, and then to the Spirit (modalism); rather, there is one

---

[26]*The Bhagavad Gita*, 11.1
[27]*The Bhagavad Gita*, 11.15-20.

God who consists of three distinct, though not separate, persons. This is what Christians call the doctrine of the Trinity.

As we reflect on the Christian view of God and His relationship to the world, we learn several important things about other aspects of the Christian worldview. Though not exhaustive, take the following:

- As a personal creator, God reveals Himself and makes Himself known to His creatures. Because of this, humans can know God in a personal way. God has made Himself known to His creatures, most especially through the incarnation of the Second Person of the Trinity.

- The reason that creation reflects unity and diversity is because the Tri-une God, who created all things, exists as three co-equal and co-eternal persons in one divine substance. Unity and diversity are metaphysical principles of the created order.

- God is the creator of all things and cares for His creation, setting the precedent for human care for the creation.

- Humans have dignity and worth because they are created in the image and likeness of God.

- The universe is rational and can be known because God is rational. God created all things by His Word and Wisdom, and His divine Wisdom is reflected in creation. Thus there is such a thing as objective truth which can be known because God has structured the universe in such a way that it is rational and knowable. Humans can know and understand the world because they were made in God's image and likeness.

- Ethics are grounded in objective reality, not only because God is the divine law giver, but because He is the ground for all morality. He is also the ground for all beauty, goodness, and truth.

- There is hope after this life because God raised Jesus from the dead, a foreshadowing of the promise to all of those who place their trust in the Judeo-Christian God, and which is also a reflection of Creation's ultimate redemption from the transience and decay of this world.

From this very brief list we see that various other worldview beliefs are interconnected to the Christian view of God and the God-world relationship.

How does our discussion in this section fit with the overall goal of the chapter? Basically, one cannot give proper attention to worldview without considering the most important element, namely, one's view of God and the God-world relation. As we saw here, there are many concepts of God. The Christian view is just but one of those. But what's important for Christians to understand is that our view of God sets the foundation for all other beliefs we have, getting back to the idea that we discussed in chapter one—everything is theological and all our beliefs come down to a theological decision. In this regard, then, our theology shapes our worldview.

Stoics, Epicureans, and the Christian Worldview: A Case Study

One way that we can gain perspective on the importance of studying worldview is by way of example. One of the clearest examples at our disposal is of the Apostle Paul's journey to Athens, as recorded by Luke in the book of Acts.

[16] Now while Paul was waiting for them at Athens, his spirit was provoked within him as he saw that the city was full of idols. [17] So he reasoned in the synagogue with the Jews and the devout persons, and in the marketplace every day with those who happened to be there. [18] Some of the Epicurean and Stoic philosophers also conversed with him. And some said, "What does this babbler wish to say?" Others said, "He seems to be a preacher of foreign divinities"—because he was preaching Jesus and the resurrection. [19] And they took him and brought him to the Areopagus, saying, "May we know what this new teaching is that you are presenting? [20] For you bring some strange things to our ears. We wish to know therefore what these things mean." [21] Now all the Athenians and the foreigners who lived there would spend their time in nothing except telling or hearing something new.

[22] So Paul, standing in the midst of the Areopagus, said: "Men of Athens, I perceive that in every way you are very religious. [23] For as I passed along and observed the objects of your worship, I found also an altar with this inscription: 'To the unknown god.' What therefore you worship as unknown, this I proclaim to you. [24] The God who made the world and everything in it, being Lord of heaven and earth, does not live in temples made by man, [25] nor is he served by human hands, as though he needed anything, since he himself gives to all mankind life and breath and everything. [26] And he made from one man every nation of mankind to live on all the face of the earth, having determined allotted periods and the boundaries of their dwelling place, [27] that they should seek God, and perhaps feel their way toward him and find him. Yet he is actually not far from each one of us, [28] for

"'In him we live and move and have our being'

as even some of your own poets have said,

"'For we are indeed his offspring.'

[29] Being then God's offspring, we ought not to think that the divine being is like gold or silver or stone, an image formed by the art and imagination of man. [30] The times of ignorance God overlooked, but now he commands all people everywhere to repent, [31] because he has fixed a day on which he will judge the world in righteousness by a man whom he has appointed; and of this he has given assurance to all by raising him from the dead." (Acts 17:16-31)

It's probable that Paul provided a much larger address than what we find recorded here. Whether that is the case or not, it's clear that Paul covers several worldview and theological issues related to God, Jesus, human beings, the world, redemption, ethics, and the afterlife. Paul understood the importance of knowing, not only his own worldview, which was shaped by his theology, but also in knowing the worldviews of others. Paul was willing to interact with the beliefs, cultures, and norms of others. As Luke tells us, Paul's "spirit was provoked" over the idolatry around him. Despite this, Paul didn't sit idly by; instead he "observed" carefully the Athenians' objects of worship. Paul engaged culture. He seized the opportunity to learn from the surrounding culture, so that he might proclaim the truth of the Christian worldview to them.

In addressing the Stoics, Epicureans, and pagans in Athens, Paul purposefully contrasted their worldviews with his own. Rather than going straight for the plan of salvation, as many Christians often to do, Paul began with the basics, that is, he began with his concept of God. There's wisdom in this. Not everyone's concept of deity is the same, and it seems from the context that Paul understood this quite well. While observing the Athenian cultic practices and objects of worship, Paul recognized an alter to "the unknown god." Taking advantage of this, Paul made a bridge to their culture by telling them about the true God. Paul argued that the God of Christianity is the transcendent Creator, who made the world and everything in it. This stands in stark contrast to the Stoics, who held to form of materialistic pantheism. Yet, against the teachings of the Epicureans, who believed that the gods (if the gods did indeed exist) had little or no concern for humans, Paul argued that people do have meaning and purpose in this life, namely to worship God. It was God who created them for such a purpose, and He's not very far from them. This shows God's immanence, Against the pagans, Paul argued that God is not made of stone, silver, or gold, nor does He dwell in temples made by human hands; rather, "God is spirit" (Jn 4:24). In other words, God is what the philosophers call "incorporeal" or "immaterial," that is, God is not made up of material stuff. As the Eternal Creator of all things, we instead owe our very existence to Him. Lastly, the center of Paul's address was on the resurrection of Christ. The resurrection, as Paul claims, is the "proof" of all that he had been claiming. The resurrection is grounded in an historical event.

As we examine Paul's method, we see that he understood the importance of majoring on the majors and avoiding getting into discussion on the finer points of theology. There's no mention of the rapture or end times, other than the fact that God is going to "judge the world . . . by a man he has appointed." Moreover, we don't see any discussion on models of the atonement or various issues related to soteriology. We do see, however, Paul zeroing in on God's call for people everywhere to repent. Paul seemingly focused on, what C. S. Lewis dubbed, a "mere Christianity." He painted a general outline of what Christians believe. That's not to say these other theological issues are unimportant. There's a time and place for such discussions. Instead, we ought to always consider our audience when presenting our worldviews. Furthermore, Paul demonstrates that despite the many differences among us, there's a core structure to the worldview shared by all Christians.

Paul wanted to see others come to a saving knowledge of the one true God. Most Christians share Paul's desire for evangelism and want to see unbelievers turn to Jesus. But Paul understood that effective evangelism requires a clear understanding of one's worldview. It may also require that we do pre-evangelism and apologetics first, challenging the presuppositions of other worldviews, while giving arguments for the truth claims the Christian faith. Moreover, for many of us, if we want to follow Paul's example, we'll need to become students of culture. Cultural engagement requires that we know not only what we believe, but also how our beliefs differ from the views of others. Therefore, it is imperative that we have a good grasp of the core teachings and doctrines of the Christian worldview.

Theology and Worldview

From this chapter we've begun to see how theology shapes a person's worldview. As stressed throughout, our understanding of God sets the foundation for many other beliefs we have. We've also begun looking at some of the other key reasons for why studying theology is important. One such reason is apologetics, to which we now turn in the next chapter.

Chapter Three

Defending the Hope Within

Apologizing for What?

If you've been a Christian for any amount of time (or if you're rather new to the Christian faith), perhaps you've heard of the word "apologetics." Contrary to how some have misconstrued the word, apologetics doesn't require Christians to go around apologizing for their faith! Rather, the task of apologetics centers on providing a reasoned defense of the Christian worldview.

"Apologetics" comes from the Greek word *apologia*, which means "defense." The noun and verb form of the word is used in the New Testament on eight different occasions (Acts 22:1; 25:16; 1 Cor 9:3; 2 Cor 7:11; Phil 1:7, 16; 2 Tim 4:16; 1 Pet 3:15). [1] In most instances, the authors use *apologia* to speak of giving a defense in a formal setting (esp. Acts 22:1; 22:16; 2 Tim 4:16), which corresponds to how the word has classically been construed in the Greek language. Here, one might think of Plato's famous *Apology of Socrates*, which tells the story of how Socrates, who was put on trial for corrupting the youth of his day, gives a defense for his actions before the people of Athens. On three occasions, Scripture uses *apologia* in connection to making a defense of the gospel (Phil 1:7, 16; 1 Pet 3:15). Perhaps, most famously, 1 Peter 3:15 gives not only a reference to the word *apologia*, but also issues a command to believers to be ready to defend the faith in the face of persecution. But what do we mean by "Christian apologetics"?

According to the Oxford dictionary, apologetics is defined as "the nature of a formal defense or justification of something such as a theory or religious doctrine." This definition is a good start, but it's a bit too generic for our purposes. While apologetics is often done in a formal setting, that doesn't always seem to be the case (e.g., 2 Cor 7:11 and 1 Pet 3:15). It's also important to note, as the definition points out, that not all apologists are Christians. As we've suggested, Plato's famous *Apology of Socrates* is an example of someone being an apologist who isn't a Christian. Other religions (e.g., Hinduism and Islam), too, have apologists. But religious folk aren't the only ones with apologists. Richard Dawkins, Sam

---

[1] James K. Beilby, *Thinking About Christian Apologetics: What It Is and Why We Do It* (Downers Grove, IL: InterVarsity Press, 2011), 12-13.

Harris, and other so-called "New Atheists," seek to give a defense of atheism and the naturalistic worldview.

We have a different aim. What we're primarily concerned with in this chapter is Christian apologetics. Therefore, let us consider another definition by philosopher Douglas Groothuis: "Christian apologetics is the rational defense of the Christian worldview as objectively true, rationally compelling and existentially or subjectively engaging."[2] Groothuis' definition has several things going for it. Firstly, it's specific to "Christian apologetics" and aimed at defending the "Christian worldview." Secondly, it places emphasis on giving a "rational defense." As discussed in the previous chapter, God has created the world in such a way that it is rational and knowable. But not everyone will agree that God is behind the orderly nature of the universe. Here, philosopher Stephen Davis is right in suggesting that we all, believer and unbeliever alike, must assume something like the rationality of the world:

> One grand presupposition . . . is that the world we experience is a cosmos rather than a chaos. That is, reality as such has a rational structure that can (at least in part) be discovered by human reason. Our rational faculties are (usually) reliable; we are capable of using them and arriving at truth.[3]

Davis wrote regarding arguments for the existence of God, but, as he reminds the reader, this is not merely a presupposition for theists alone. The entire enterprise of scientific and philosophical thinking rests on presupposing the rationality of our universe. He continues, "Of course, critics of theistic proofs . . . make this assumption about the order and intelligibility of the world too; indeed, so does everyone who wants to argue rationally for some conclusion or another."[4] Thirdly, what we're arguing for is "objectively true," that is to say, it's not a matter of opinion or feelings; rather, the truth claims of Christianity can be tested and verified. I may believe that the moon is made up of green cheese. Despite my intentions, just because I believe that it's true doesn't make it true. Fourthly, we should never appeal to force (which is an informal logical fallacy) in our argumentation; instead, our arguments should be "rationally compelling." Fifthly, and lastly, what we're defending should be "existentially engaging," that is to say, our views that we're defending should be such that they speak to all of life and are livable. What good would defending such a worldview be if we can't live out the implications of our beliefs.

To further our understanding of apologetics, we can think of our task in two ways—*offensive apologetics* and *defensive apologetics*. When a sports team is on the defense, it aims to keep the other team from scoring points. When a sports team is on the offense, its primary goal surrounds gaining points. Just as any

---

[2]Douglas Groothuis, *Christian Apologetics: A Comprehensive Case for Biblical Faith* (Downers Grove, IL: InterVarsity Press, 2011), 24.

[3]Stephen T. Davis, *God, Reason and Theistic Proofs* (Grand Rapids, MI: Wm B. Eerdmans Publishing Company, 1997), 8.

[4]Ibid.

sports team has an offense and a defense, something similar is required of those engaging in apologetics.

Let me be clear. Apologetics isn't about scoring points. Our purpose isn't about winning arguments, nor is it about getting another soul notch in our prover-bial soul-winning belts. It's not about us at all! Surely, we do want to see people repent and turn to the Lord, but not for the *mere* sake of winning souls. Let's think about it like this. Suppose we have a cure for an awful disease. Should we stand around with the cure without telling others? By no means! We should do all that we can to get the cure out to others. Let's pull back and think about how this applies to the task of apologetics. Before his ascension, Jesus commanded His followers to go into all the world and make disciples. In so doing, they are to teach them all that He had commanded, and they are to be baptized in the name of the triune God (Mt 28:19-20). The emphasis here is on "making disciples," but making disciples often includes the task of evangelism. In other words, we are to proclaim the gospel—the good news. But sometimes evangelism (and making disciples, I might add) requires apologetics. In that sense, apologetics compli-ments the dual tasks of evangelism and disciple-making.

So, what then do we mean by "offensive" and "defensive" apologetics, if it doesn't have anything to do with scoring points? James Beilby provides a help-ful way of thinking through the difference between the two. Instead of using the words "offensive" and "defensive," Beilby focuses rather on, what he calls, "pro-active" and "responsive" apologetics. The purpose of proactive (offensive) apolo-getics is to demonstrate the truthfulness or rationality of the Christian faith. He breaks proactive apologetics down into two forms: (1) "constructive arguments," which focus on the truthfulness of the Christian faith; and (2) "deconstructive arguments," which places emphasis on showing other worldviews as false. In the same way, responsive (defensive) apologetics, which shows arguments against the Christian faith are unsuccessful, comes in two forms: (1) "rebutting argu-ments," which place emphasis on responding to an objection raised against the Christian faith; and (2) "undercutting arguments," which aim to show that there's something wrong with the objection itself.

Biblical Case for Apologetics

So far, we've seen how the word "apologetics" is used in the New Testament, and we've considered the nature of apologetics, but some of you might still be won-dering whether apologetics is biblical? Why should anyone engage in apologet-ics? As we'll see, the Bible has quite a bit to say about the discipline of apologet-ics. To be clear, in most instances, the word *apologia* is never used, but like many Christian doctrines, the concept is found throughout the entirety of the Bible. Furthermore, while we can't look at all passages related to apologetics, we'll con-sider only the key data from both the Old and New Testaments.

The Old Testament

One will look high and low to find a definitive passage in the Old Testament charging the saints with the task of defending the faith. But, of course, that doesn't mean there are no relevant passages. As we'll see below, apologetics began in the beginning. Not the beginning of the universe; rather, we see it taking place in the first chapters of the Bible.

Old Testament scholars have long recognized the first chapters of Genesis as a polemic against Israel's neighbors.[5] Israel had just come out of Egypt, a land plagued (no pun intended) with a pantheon of gods and goddesses. For the Egyptian worldview, as was the case with many nations surrounding Israel, the gods were central figures in their creation myths. The first chapters of Genesis present a different kind of story from what the Israelites were used to hearing from their pagan neighbors, especially their Egyptian captors, and it was meant as a corrective to those false views. Consider the words of Old Testament scholar, Gordon H. Johnston:

> Genesis 1 appears to be a literary polemic designed to refute ancient Near Eastern creation mythology in general, but ancient Egyptian creation mythology in particular. Although there are several elements in this passage which surely reflect a general Semitic background, the majority of parallel elements are cast against the Egyptian mythologies. This suggests that Genesis 1 was originally composed . . as a theological polemic against the ancient Egyptian models of creation which competed against Yahwism for the loyalty of the ancient Israelites.[6]

Genesis 1 isn't the only place we find apologetics in the Old Testament. The writers of the Old Testament record God's mighty acts throughout salvation history. Most significantly we find God's deliverance of Israel from the clutches of the Egyptians. The Israelites, God's chosen people, had been held in captivity by the Egyptians for four hundred years when they were finally freed. But the Israelites' freedom didn't come about through political upheaval or rebellion from their captors; rather, it came about through God's supernatural working and displaying of His awesome power. This is especially true with respect to the plagues sent against Egypt for Pharaohs' refusal to let the Israelites go. Consider the following passages:

Exodus 7:1-5

And the Lord said to Moses, "See, I have made you like God to Pharaoh, and your

---

[5]For a helpful overview of many of the parallels and central differences between Genesis One and the pagan creation myths of Israel's neighbors, see Johnny V. Miller and John M. Soden, *In the Beginning . . . We Misunderstood: Interpreting Genesis 1 in Its Original Context* (Grand Rapids, MI: Kregel Publications, 2012). For an important study into the ancient cosmology of Genesis One, see John H. Walton, *The Lost World of Genesis One: Ancient Cosmology and the Origins Debate* (Downers Grove, IL: InterVarsity Press, 2009).

[6]Gordon H. Johnston, "Genesis 1 and Ancient Egyptian Creation Myths," *Bibliotheca Sacra* 165, no. 2 (April-June 2008), 194.

brother Aaron shall be your prophet. ² You shall speak all that I command you, and your brother Aaron shall tell Pharaoh to let the people of Israel go out of his land. ³ But I will harden Pharaoh's heart, and though I multiply my signs and wonders in the land of Egypt, ⁴ Pharaoh will not listen to you. Then I will lay my hand on Egypt and bring my hosts, my people the children of Israel, out of the land of Egypt by great acts of judgment. ⁵ The Egyptians shall know that I am the Lord, when I stretch out my hand against Egypt and bring out the people of Israel from among them."

Exodus 9:14-17

¹⁴ For this time I will send all my plagues on you yourself, and on your servants and your people, so that you may know that there is none like me in all the earth. ¹⁵ For by now I could have put out my hand and struck you and your people with pestilence, and you would have been cut off from the earth. ¹⁶ But for this purpose I have raised you up, to show you my power, so that my name may be proclaimed in all the earth. ¹⁷ You are still exalting yourself against my people and will not let them go.

Exodus 12:12-13

¹² For I will pass through the land of Egypt that night, and I will strike all the firstborn in the land of Egypt, both man and beast; and on all the gods of Egypt I will execute judgments: I am the LORD. ¹³ The blood shall be a sign for you, on the houses where you are. And when I see the blood, I will pass over you, and no plague will befall you to destroy you, when I strike the land of Egypt.

As we examine each of these passages, several themes emerge. First, it is by God's mighty acts that He brings about His judgment on Pharaoh and the Egyptians for their refusal to let the Israelites go. In so doing, God will bring freedom to His people. However, this results in a second theme—the Egyptians will come to understand that the God of Israel is the one true God. Third, through His mighty acts, the name of Israel's God will be proclaimed throughout the nations. Fourth, it is through God's might acts that He executes judgment against the gods of Egypt. Fifth, and lastly, God's mighty work brings assurance to the Israelites that He is, indeed, the one true God.

Another important event, which reflects God's mighty acts, includes Elijah and the Prophets of Baal. On Mount Carmel, Elijah challenges the people of Israel to stop teetering between "two different opinions." He then goes on to say, "If the LORD is God follow him; but if Baal, then follow him" (1 Kgs 18:21). Elijah is giving the people of Israel an ultimatum. Interesting enough, he's also applying one of the main laws of logic—the law of non-contradiction. He recognizes that it would be a contradiction to serve both Yahweh and Baal. The people needed to choose one or other, since both can't be the true God. As the story unwinds, Elijah and the prophets of Baal each form two altars with a sacrifice. They've agreed to call on their deity, and whichever God—Yahweh or Baal—answers by fire is the true God. The author of 1 Kings tells us that the prophets called on Baal until noon. At one point, they began slashing themselves. The prophets continued with this until evening. Elijah then called the spectators over to him. He repaired the alter, dug a trench around it, and had the people observing to fill four large water jars and pour it all over the alter. Afterwards, Elijah called on the LORD and immediately fire came down from heaven burning up, not only the sacrifice, but also the wood, stones, soil, and water from the trench. When the people of Israel saw what had happened, they fell down on their faces and proclaimed that the LORD is God.

The Exodus event and what took place on Mount Carmel with the prophets of Baal are just two examples of many in the Bible where God used men (e.g., Moses and Elijah) and women to be instruments for displaying His mighty acts to the world. God doesn't need humans to accomplish His purposes; nevertheless, He chooses to use them.

The New Testament

Having considered evidence from the Old Testament, we now turn to apologetics in the New Testament. In what follows, we'll consider Jesus and Paul as apologists, followed by various other key New Testament passages on apologetics.

Most people, when they think of Jesus, don't consider Him to be an apologist. But as we look at His life more closely, we see that Jesus was engaged in apologetics throughout His three-and-a-half years of ministry. We find Him challenging authority (Mt 21:23-27), offering testimony on His behalf in defense of His ministry (Mt 5:17; Mk 1:11; Jn 1:29; 5:33-46; 8:14), using fulfilled prophecy (Lk 7:19-23), engaging in debate with logic and reasoned argument (Mt 12:9-14, 22-28; 22:15-22, 23-32; Jn 7:21-24; 10:24-41), and giving evidences (Jn 20:26-29)—especially through signs and miracles (Jn 5:36; 10:24-25, 38).[7]

Jesus' apologetic ministry culminated with His resurrection from the dead, whereby God vindicated Him and authenticated His message. The resurrection functioned as the catalyst for early Christian worship of Jesus[8] and stands as the pinnacle of Christian theology.[9] On multiple occasions, Jesus predicted His own resurrection (Mt 12:38-40; 16:1-4; 17:22-23; 20:18-19; Mk 8:31-32; 10:33-34;

---

[7]For a helpful study on Jesus as an apologist, see Norman L. Geisler and Patrick Zukeran, *The Apologetics of Jesus: A Caring Approach to Dealing with Doubters* (Grand Rapids, MI: Baker Books, 2009).

[8]For an excellent study on early Jesus worship, see Larry W. Hurtado's *How on Earth Did Jesus Become a God?: Historical Questions about Earliest Devotion to Jesus* (Grand Rapids, MI: Wm. B. Eerdmans Publishing Co., 2005). For a more detailed work, consider Hurtado's *Lord Jesus Christ: Devotion to Jesus in Earliest Christianity* (Grand Rapids, MI: Eerdmans, 2005). Similarly, see Richard Bauckham, *Jesus and the God of Israel: God Crucified and Other Studies on the New Testament's Christology of Divine Identity* (Grand Rapids, MI: Eerdmans, 2008).

[9]Gary R. Habermas has argued for this point extensively in *The Risen Jesus and Future Hope* (Lanham, MD: Rowman and Littlefield Publishers, 2003).

Lk 98:22; Jn 2:18-21). Moreover, the resurrection itself was the fulfillment of prophecy (Is 53:8-10; Mt 26:31-35; Lk 24:44).[10] The climax of Peter's argument in his Acts 2 sermon hung on the predictions made by King David in Psalm 16:8-11. Note Peter's words:

[24] God raised him up, loosing the pangs of death, because it was not possible for him to be held by it. [25] For David says concerning him," 'I saw the Lord always before me,

for he is at my right hand that I may not be shaken;

[26] therefore my heart was glad, and my tongue rejoiced;

my flesh also will dwell in hope.

[27] For you will not abandon my soul to Hades,

or let your Holy One see corruption.

[28] You have made known to me the paths of life;

you will make me full of gladness with your presence.'

[29] "Brothers, I may say to you with confidence about the patriarch David that he both died and was buried, and his tomb is with us to this day. [30] Being therefore a prophet, and knowing that God had sworn with an oath to him that he would set one of his descendants on his throne, [31] he foresaw and spoke about the resurrection of the Christ, that he was not abandoned to Hades, nor did his flesh see corruption. [32] This Jesus God raised up, and of that we all are witnesses. (Acts 2:24-32)

Even before His resurrection, Jesus made the following claim about himself:

"I am the resurrection and the life. Whoever believes in me, though he die, yet shall he live, [26] and everyone who lives and believes in me shall never die." (Jn 11:25-26)

With this passage in mind, Norman Geisler and Patrick Zukeran summarize well the importance of Jesus' resurrection:

Jesus claims to be the source of life and the victor over physical death. Many "saviors" may make this claim, but in the unique event of his resurrection, Jesus alone confirms his claim. The founders of all religions have died, but Christ alone predicted his death, burial, and resurrection and accomplished this feat.[11]

The Apostle Paul, too, engaged in apologetics. One need only to look to his missionary journeys in Acts to find Luke, the author of Acts, using such words as "reasoned," "explaining," "proving," "testifying," "expounded," and "trying to convince" to describe Paul's ministry (Acts 17:1-4, 16-17, 18:5, and 28:23). Paul

---

[10]Geisler and Zukeran, *The Apologetics of Jesus*, 57-63.
[11]Ibid., 62.

often used fulfilled prophecy (Acts 13:16-52) and reasoned from the Scriptures when ministering to the Jews. Take, for example, the following passage:

> [17] Now when they had passed through Amphipolis and Apollonia, they came to Thessalonica, where there was a synagogue of the Jews. [2] And Paul went in, as was his custom, and on three Sabbath days he reasoned with them from the Scriptures, [3] explaining and proving that it was necessary for the Christ to suffer and to rise from the dead, and saying, "This Jesus, whom I proclaim to you, is the Christ." [4] And some of them were persuaded and joined Paul and Silas, as did a great many of the devout Greeks and not a few of the leading women. (Acts 17:1-4)

There's much we can learn from this passage about Paul's apologetic method:

- Paul had a specific target audience in mind, namely, the Jews

- Paul understood his target audience well and used the method he considered to be most effective in reaching them

- Paul's method consisted of reasoning with the Jews from the Scriptures

- Paul's aim was to show why it was necessary for the Christ to suffer and rise from the dead

Let's contrast Paul's method here with his apologetic approach in Acts 17:16-34. I'll not rehash all that went down, since we considered this passage extensively in the previous chapter; rather, I'll highlight for our purposes only those main points of Paul's method in ministering to the people of Athens:

- Paul understood his audience, which consisted of Epicurean and Stoic philosophers and pagans

- Paul observed the surrounding culture, looking for areas of common ground or touching off points (e.g., quoting from Greek poets and philosophers, using the altar with the inscription: TO AN UNKNOWN GOD)

- Paul compared his understanding of deity and the core tenets of his worldview with those of his audience

- Paul emphasized the use of evidence by appealing to the resurrection

As we compare the two passages, we see similarities and differences. Let's consider some similarities. In both passages, we see that Paul had a clear understanding of the people to whom he was ministering. Furthermore, in both passages, we see that Paul used reason and evidence in effort to win over his audiences to the truth. Despite these similarities, there significant differences persist. With the Jews, Paul shared a common heritage and sacred text—the Old Testament Scriptures. Furthermore, he shared with them a common understanding of God. The Jews were expecting a Messiah, someone who would be God's anointed deliverer. Paul's chief aim was to build an argument from the Scriptures for why the Christ had to suffer and rise again and to show Jesus was, indeed, this Messiah. Paul didn't share the same background information with the Epicureans, Stoics, and pagans. He had to start from scratch. His objective centered on first building an argument for a certain understanding of God and then to move to evidence to support the particulars of the Christian worldview, placing emphasis on the resurrection. In both cases, God used Paul's apologetic efforts to bring others to Himself.

There's much we can learn from Jesus and Paul. Both were exemplar apologists. But there's additional New Testament support for why Christians should engage in the task of apologetics. As James Beilby stresses, the Gospels themselves were written with an apologetics focus:

> [T]he Gospels have a particular clear apologetic focus. Most of them center on demonstrating that the life, death and resurrection of Jesus fulfilled a whole range of Old Testament prophecies. The first concerns the origins of Jesus. In the Jewish tradition it was clear that the Messiah must be in King David's royal line. Consequentially, Gospel writers, particularly those writing to a Jewish audience, were concerned to demonstrate that Jesus was in David's line (as required by 2 Sam 7:12-13; Ps 89:3-4; 132:11-12; and Dan 9:25) and that he was born in Bethlehem (as required by Mic 5:2). The second concerns the widespread failure of the Jews to recognize Jesus as Messiah. All four Gospel writers (and Luke in Acts 28:26-27) answer the charge by citing Isaiah 6:10, which asserts that God himself blinded those who listened to Isaiah and prevented them from understanding.[12]

Other key apologetics texts include:

2 Corinthians 10:5

"We destroy arguments and every lofty opinion raised against the knowledge of God, and take every thought captive to obey Christ"

Jude 3

"Beloved, although I was very eager to write to you about our common salvation, I found it necessary to write appealing to you to contend for the faith that was once for all delivered to the saints."

1 Peter 3:15

"but in your hearts honor Christ the Lord as holy, always being prepared to make a defense to anyone who asks you for a reason for the hope that is in you; yet do it with gentleness and respect"

The Aim of Apologetics

Each of the above verses give insight into the task of apologetics. For our purposes, we're going to unpack 1 Peter 3:15 a bit more, which will not only give us insights into the task of the apologist, but will also illuminate the important

---

[12]Beilby, *Thinking About Christian Apologetics*, 38-39.

relationship between theology and apologetics. Let's consider each section, beginning with "but in your hearts honor Christ the Lord as holy."

When the biblical authors of Scripture used the word "heart," they obviously didn't mean our physical organ; rather, it's a reference to the center of who we are as humans. It is the core of our being—our intellectual, emotional, and moral core. Consider what Jesus said about the heart in Luke 6:45:

> The good person out of the good treasure of his heart produces good, and the evil person out of his evil treasure produces evil, for out of the abundance of the heart his mouth speaks.

Elsewhere, in Matthew 15:18, he says the following:

> But what comes out of the mouth proceeds from the heart, and this defiles a person. For out of the heart come evil thoughts, murder, adultery, sexual immorality, theft, false witness, and slander. These are what defile a person. But to eat with unwashed hands does not defile anyone.

What comes out of our mouths says a lot about who we are. In the passage we're investigating, Peter highlights the fact that when Christians engage in the task of apologetics, the heart matters. We need to keep our intentions in check. Sadly, some people think that apologetics is only about besting our opponents through presenting these knock-down-drag-out arguments. But that's a misconstrued understanding of apologetics. The task of the apologist is never about winning an argument. Peter is writing to a group of people who were being persecuted for their faith. They weren't concerned about winning an argument but for their very lives. Rather, he's emphasizing the need to stand firm in their faith during persecution and to be faithful witnesses for Christ. The task of apologetics, then, is about helping a person move closer to Jesus. We want to see people move from darkness to light. Ultimately, when we engage in apologetics, we want to bring glory to Jesus, not to ourselves. We want to make sure that our hearts are right as we reflect Jesus to the world. We do what we do for the sake of Christ, and we want to honor Him through our efforts in apologetics. All our actions, then, should be set apart to honor our Lord.

As we continue to make our way through this important passage on apologetics, we next consider "always be prepared to make a defense." Again, those to whom Peter is writing are facing persecution for their faith. He's instructing his readers to "always be prepared." We've all experienced times, whether in our evangelistic attempts or from our friends and family, when someone's asked a question regarding our faith that we simply couldn't answer. Or, if we gave an answer, we didn't feel as if we answered it sufficiently. That's okay! We've all been there before. As we reflect on Peter's command, it may be helpful to consider some "tools" of the apologist.

People skilled in a trade know that to complete the job well they need the right tools. Even if they don't have the proper tools, they know where to get them. In the same way, when we engage in the task of apologetics, there's some tools we need in order to do our job well. The first tool is having a good grasp of Christian doctrine. This is where theology comes in. After all, what we're defending is the faith itself, that is, the core Christian doctrines that have been handed down to us from Jesus and the apostles (1 Cor 15: 3; Jude 3). As someone who has a Ph.D. in theology, I can assure you that I don't know all there is to know about theology. I don't always have the answers. I'm sure, at times, you don't either. Thankfully, we're not called to perfection in our answers! But we are called to be ready to make a defense. To do this, we must have a good grasp of what Christians believe. This, however, leads to the second tool—the ability to know why we believe what we do. This is where apologetics comes in. It's not enough to know "what" we believe, but we must also need to know "why" we believe it. When we're faced with questions and doubts about the Christian faith, we need to be prepared. That's not to say that there's going to be times where we don't have the answers. But just as skilled tradespeople know where to get the tools they need, Christians need to know where to get the answers to those tough questions. Sometimes, we must step back, do some study, and then follow up with our interlocutors. It's alright to tell people that you don't have the answer right now and that you'll get back to them on their questions. Unfortunately, we're not always going to have the opportunity to go back and study. That's why it's so important that we begin studying theology and apologetics now. We need to be ready and prepared!

A third tool is having a good understanding of logic. You'd be surprised how far a little logic will go in helping you to become a clearer thinker and in recognizing arguments. Fourth, learn basic logical fallacies. It's surprising how often we run into logical fallacies, whether on Facebook or social media, in the news, from Presidential candidates, friends, neighbors, and in our own thinking!

Moving along, Peter tells us that we're to make a defense "to anyone who asks." On the one hand, we are to be ready to give a defense to unbelievers, whether skeptics, atheists and agnostics, or people of other faiths. It would be a mistake, however, to think that we should only do apologetics with unbelievers. Many believers have doubts. Growing up in church, I often heard that real Christians don't have doubts. Perhaps, many of you have heard this too. But anyone who's spent time in the Bible realizes that many of our heroes of the faith were plagued with doubts. Abraham and Sarah, Moses, Elijah, John the Baptist, James (the half-brother of Jesus—who was a skeptic about his brother until after the resurrection), Thomas, Peter, and Paul all had their bouts with doubt. But when we look at the pages of the Scriptures, we see that once those doubts were removed, they went on to do great things for the Lord. Perhaps, one of the most neglected areas of apologetics is in working with our friends, family members, and fellow brothers and sisters at church who are struggling with doubt (we'll consider this more fully in a later chapter). Another area to consider when working with believers centers on coherence arguments. There are certain Christian doctrines that are difficult to understand, especially those pertaining to the Trinity, incarnation, Christ's atonement for sins, God's relationship to the world, and the attributes of God. Sometimes brothers and sisters in Christ need help understanding these doctrines. They need to be shown how they are coherent and without contradiction.

When dialoguing with unbelievers, we shouldn't assume that they're uninterested or that they aren't sincere in asking the questions they do. Sometimes unbelievers have good questions and genuinely want to know answers. When their questions are answered, they may not become Christians, but God may use the removal of a doubt to plant a seed. For all we know, it may be the beginning of a paradigm shift in their thinking.

Not only is Peter challenging his readers to give a defense of the faith, but they are also to provide "a reason for the hope" that's in them. Have you ever reflected on that, that is, that we have hope? When we think of something as awful as cancer or other life-threatening diseases, if someone were to tell us they had the cure, it would be an amazing thing. It would mean the difference between life and death. In the same way, as we engage in the task of defending the faith, we have a life-changing message that is grounded in the hope found in our Lord and Savior, Jesus! He is the one who rose from the grave, conquering death. He defeated the one enemy that affects us all. The hope that we have is found in Him and His message, namely, that God is going to do in us what He did in Jesus. We, too, will one day be raised with a new body. As Paul tells us in his first letter to the Corinthians, our perishable, mortal bodies will be clothed with immortality, never to perish again, because "Death is swallowed up in victory" (1 Cor 15:54). Moreover, the Apostle John has much to say about our future hope:

> Then I saw a new heaven and a new earth, for the first heaven and the first earth had passed away, and the sea was no more. ² And I saw the holy city, new Jerusalem, coming down out of heaven from God, prepared as a bride adorned for her husband. ³ And I heard a loud voice from the throne saying, "Behold, the dwelling place of God is with man. He will dwell with them, and they will be his people, and God himself will be with them as their God. ⁴ He will wipe away every tear from their eyes, and death shall be no more, neither shall there be mourning, nor crying, nor pain anymore, for the former things have passed away." ⁵ And he who was seated on the throne said, "Behold, I am making all things new." (Rev 21:1-5)

What a powerful vision of God's goal for the created order. In the new heavens and in the new earth there will be no more pain, suffering, or sorrow. God himself will be present among us. No longer will we weep, or cry, or experience death. Those things will be gone because God is in the process of making all things new. This new order is the result of the work of our great and glorious Lord, who not only saved us from our sin, but who has also given us His Spirit, who now indwells all who are in Christ, transforming us and moving us toward God's glorious eschatological goal. God is making all things new, and He is inviting us all to be a part of it!

Lastly, Peter tells his readers to give a defense with "gentleness and respect." As we engage others, whether believers or unbelievers, we are to demonstrate Christ-likeness in all that we do. As noted earlier, our primary goal isn't to win an argument. Our goal isn't even to win people to the Lord—it's the Holy Spirit's role to work on them and to use what we do to win them. Our goal is to be faithful in the task that God has called us to and to present truth to those who are in need of Christ's redeeming work. Yet, we're to accomplish our task with "gentleness and respect," as Christ's ambassadors (2 Cor 5:20). We should always keep before us Jesus' command to love our neighbors as ourselves (Mk 12:31).

The Daily Task of Apologetics

You might be wondering: "How might the task of apologetics look on a day-to-day basis?" Perhaps, looking at some misconceptions might help. One misconception is the idea that defending the faith must take place in a formal manner, whether in a church pulpit, conference center, or some other formal setting. But that's not the case at all. Sometimes the most important apologetic work we do takes place in our homes, work, social interactions with people, churches, or coffee shops. Another misconception, which I've touched on a bit already, is the idea that we must know everything to be effective apologists. Sometimes it's just a matter of starting a conversation with a friend, family member, or stranger to get the dialogue going. Apologist Greg Koukl shares a story in his book, *Tactics*, about starting up a conversation with women just by asking her whether her necklace had any religious significance. As it turns out, it did, and they entered a longer conversation just because he asked her a question.[13]

Having considered two misconceptions, another way that we can do apologetics on a day-to-day basis is by answering questions that people have about the faith. If you have children, take the time to hear their questions. If you work in a youth group, find out what students are listening to or watching on T.V., or engage with them through social media. Ask them questions about the worldviews that are present through such means and help them to compare those worldviews with the Christian worldview.[14] Perhaps you're a pastor. Begin doing more apologetic sermons or Bible studies to help your folks learn how to think apologetically and to engage culture. If you know people struggling with doubt, help them to answer their theological questions. No matter where you are, there's always places to engage people in apologetics. Sometimes it's just in our everyday living!

Theology and Apologetics

The heart of this chapter centered on Christian apologetics. The chapter began by offering a brief overview of the nature of apologetics, followed by a biblical case for why Christians should engage in apologetics. We also considered the relationship between theology as we examined 1 Peter 3:15 and the task of the apologetics. Finally, we looked at what it means to be an apologist daily. Hopefully from this chapter you've begun to see the important relationship between theology and apologetics. In the next chapter, we're going to continue our discussion on apologetics and theology, but with emphasis on guarding against false teaching.

---

[13]Greg Koukl, *Tactics: A Game Plan for Discussing Your Christian Convictions* (Grand Rapids, MI: Zondervan, 2009.

[14]For a helpful introduction, I recommend Walt Mueller, *Understanding Today's Youth Culture: A Complete Guide for Parents, Teachers, and Youth Leaders* (Wheaton, IL: Tyndale, 1999).

Chapter Four

Correcting False Teaching

I believe in God, the Father almighty, creator of heaven and earth.

I believe in Jesus Christ, God's only Son, our Lord, who was conceived by the Holy Spirit, born of a Virgin Mary, suffered under Pontius Pilate, was crucified, died, and was buried; he descended to the dead. On the third day he rose again; he ascended into heaven, he is seated at the right hand of the Father, and he will come again to judge the living and the dead.

I believe in the Holy Spirit, the holy catholic church, the communion of saints, the forgiveness of sins, the resurrection of the body, and the life everlasting. AMEN.[1]

Credo: "I Believe"

The Apostles' Creed hails as one of the oldest summaries of Christian belief. Each of the three major branches of Christianity—Catholics, Orthodox, and Protestants—accept it as a basic statement of what all Christians hold true,[2] though there are some minor disagreements on the wording of the creed.[3] The creed's origin remains unclear, and it is highly doubtful the twelve apostles composed the creed, though tradition suggests that each of the major articles were attributed to them.[4] The Trinitarian shape to the creed, along with its succinct nature, indicates that it was most likely used as an ancient baptismal confession.[5]

Creeds have long been a part of the Christian church. Those who recited creeds in the early church didn't take their words lightly, as Thomas C. Oden explains:

---

[1]"The Apostles' Creed," Creeds of Christendom, accessed February 15, 2017, https://www.creeds.net/ancient/apostles.htm

[2]Other "ecumenical" creeds accepted by most Christians include the Nicen Creed (325), the Constantinopolitan Creed (351), the Chalcedonian Creed (451), and the Athanasian Creed (c. 500).

[3]For example, should the creed say, "descended into Hell" instead of "descended to the dead," or should the phrase be in there at all, since some versions omit it. "Communion of saints" is also a contested part of the creed.

[4]"The Apostles' Creed," in *The Christian Theology* Reader, 4th ed., ed. Alister McGrath (Malden, MA: Wiley-Blackwell, 2011), 11.

[5]Thomas C. Oden, *Classic Christianity: A Systematic Theology* (New York: HarperOne, 1992), 9-10.

Christians who first said credo ("I believe") did not do so lightly, but at the risk of their lives under severe persecution. We listen carefully to those who are prepared to sacrifice their lives for their belief. To say credo genuinely is to speak from the heart, to reveal who one is by confessing one's essential belief, the faith that makes life worth living. One who says credo without willingness to suffer and if necessary die, for the faith has not yet genuinely said credo.[6]

As succinct statements of Christian belief, creeds have served the purpose of teaching basic Christian doctrine within the church, guarding orthodoxy (true belief) against heretical (false) teaching, and expressing worship within the service.

Though not widely recognized outside of scholarly circles, the New Testament itself contains forty-to-fifty so-called "hymns" or "creeds",[7] most of which were directed toward Jesus.[8] Despite some obvious differences between the two, scholars aren't always clear whether a confession found within the New Testament is a hymn or a creed. The most widely recognized New Testament hymns and creeds include: Romans 1:3b-4; 3:24-26; 10:9-10; I Corinthians 8:6; 15:3b-5; Gal 3:26-28; 4:4-5; Philippians 2:6-11; 1 Timothy 3:16b; Hebrews 1:3; Colossians 1:15-18; 1 Peter 2:22-23; and John's prologue.[9] New Testament scholar Oscar Cullman suggests that these early confessional statements served five basic purposes within the New Testament church: "baptism and catecumenism," "worship," "exorcism," "persecution," and "polemics against heretics."[10]

New Testament creeds and hymns allow modern readers to peer inside the worship services of the early church. Passages such as 1 Corinthians 14:26, Colossians 3:16-17, and Ephesians 18b-20 suggest that the early church regularly included "psalms," "hymns," "spiritual songs," and "singing making melody" in their worship services. Upon a cursory examination, it doesn't take much to see that these early Christian confessional statements contain theologically rich material. The often rhythmic and pithy nature of such creeds and hymns served as a mnemonic device for retention of core Christian doctrine amongst a largely oral culture. New Testament confessional material functioned as a way of preserving the pure doctrine of the early church, and was meant to be passed on to preserve the faith (1 Cor 11:23; 15:1-3; Jude 3).

It didn't take long before false teaching began infiltrating the freshly minted church. From the time of the apostles on, Christians have combated false teaching, seeking to hold firmly to the faith handed down to them from Jesus and the

---

[6]Ibid., 8.

[7]Richard N. Longnecker, "Christological Materials in the Early Christian Communities," in *Contours of Christology in the New Testament*, edited by Richard N. Longenecker (Grand Rapids, MI: William B. Eerdmans Publishing Company, 2005), 71.

[8]Oscar Cullmann, *The Earliest Christian Confessions*, trans. J. K. S. Reid (London: Lutterworth Press, 1949), 38; Vernon H. Neufeld, *The Earliest Christian Confessions* (Grand Rapids, MI: Wm B. Eerdmans, 1963), 21.

[9]Longenecker, "Christological Materials in the Early Christian Communities," 71; Martin Hengel, "The Song about Christ in Earliest Worship," in *Studies in Early Christology* (Edinburgh: T &T Clark, 1995), 285.

[10]Cullmann, *The Earliest Christian Confessions*, 18.

apostles (Jude 3). In this chapter, we're going to take a closer look at false teaching in the New Testament, false teaching in the early church, and false teaching today. Before we turn there, we must carefully consider key terms, making proper distinctions between words such as "orthodox," "heresy," "religion," "sect," "denomination," "cult," and the "occult."

Orthodoxy and Heresy

You may have heard the saying "Christianity is a relationship, not a religion." There's some truth to that, but it needs some unpacking. Those who use this phrase mean that Christianity isn't merely some religious activity that we engage in. It's not merely a bunch of "dos" and "don'ts," a collection of religious teachings, or an ethical system by which we abide (though it may very well include those); rather, it's about a personal God reaching down to a fallen and broken creation, rescuing it from sin and destruction through the redeeming work of the raised incarnate Son of God and through the empowering regenerative work of the Holy Spirit. The eternal Creator God enters into a redemptive relationship with those who believe, granting them eternal/abundant life by His grace, apart from their own efforts. In this sense, Christianity differs from other religions. Christianity is deeply rooted in the concept of grace. Rather than humans making their way to God, God initiates the salvation process, reaching down to us, and providing the means for our salvation.

There is a second, more technical way of understanding the word "religion." Roger Schmidt et al. define religion as "systems of meaning embodied in a pattern of life, a community of faith, and a worldview that articulate a view of the sacred and of what ultimately matters."[11] In other words, common beliefs and practices, views on ultimate meaning and purpose, and an understanding of the sacred all unite a group of people. In this more descriptive sense of the word, Christianity classifies as a "religion," as does Judaism, Islam, Buddhism, Taoism, Shinto, Hinduism, and Sikhism, just to name a few.

Religions and worldviews have much in common, though, there are some differences between the two. Religions ascribe a sacredness to life and see their way of understanding reality as providing ultimate significance and meaning. That isn't always the case with certain nontheistic worldviews (e.g., naturalism, atheism, and humanism). Though, nontheistic as it may be, some naturalists have advanced a movement toward, what they call, "religious naturalism," whereby they ascribe to the belief that nature itself is sacred.[12] Such an understanding shares certain af-

---

[11]Roger Schmidt et al., *Patterns of Religion* (Belmont, CA: Wadsworth, 1999), 10 as quoted in Gerald R. McDermott and Harold A. Netland, *A Trinitarian Theology of Religions: An Evangelical Proposal* (New York: Oxford University Press, 2014), 233.

[12]For recent attempts, see Donald A. Crosby, *Nature as Sacred Ground: A Metaphysics for Religious Naturalism*, reprint ed. (Albany, NY: State University of New York Press, 2016); Loyal Rue, *Nature is Enough: Religious Naturalism and the Meaning of Life* (Albany, NY: State University of New York Press, 2011); Jerome A. Stone, *Religious Naturalism Today: The Rebirth of a Forgotten Alternative* (Albany, NY: State University of New

finities to pantheism, though religious naturalists would not classify themselves as "pantheistic," since they do not ascribe to a concept of the divine.[13] Perhaps, in the sense described here, naturalism, too, might qualify as a religion—though, not all naturalists would want that label.

Within any given religion, there are also *branches, sects,* and *denominations.* We've already pointed out three main branches of Christianity: Catholicism, Orthodox, and Protestantism. I've heard some people classify Catholicism as a different religion, or they make a distinction between Christians and Catholics. That's not quite right. All three groups belong under the heading of "Christianity," though there certainly are important differences between each group. Denomination, on the other hand, refers to a group within a branch of a religion. For example, Baptists, Presbyterians, Lutherans, Methodists, and Episcopalians all classify as denominational families within Protestant Christianity. Within denominational families, further divisions often occur. Among Baptists, for example, there are Free Will Baptists, Southern Baptists, Converge Worldwide (formally Baptist General Conference), and American Baptists. These divisions, too, can appropriately be labeled "denominations." Generally, denominational affiliation, particularly in Christianity, places focus on certain teachings, often on secondary issues of the faith, such as church polity (how churches are governed) or the nature of baptism (believer's baptism or infant baptism). The word "sect," while often functioning similarly to "denomination" in many religious contexts, refers (particularly in Christianity) to a lesser known offshoot of a denomination. Certain sects are often exclusivist in nature and place improper emphasis on a singular doctrine or teaching—such abuses of doctrines are known as aberrations.

So far, we've looked at the differences between a religion, a religious branch, a denomination, and a sect, but there are four other key terms that need fleshing out: orthodoxy, heresy, cult, and occult. Let's begin by considering the difference between orthodoxy and heresy.

The term "orthodoxy" refers to the true or right teaching of the Church, or one might think of the "rule of faith" (Jude 3) that's been passed down to us from Jesus and the apostles. Justin Holcomb defines it this way: "Orthodoxy is the teaching that best follows the Bible and best summarizes what it teaches."[14] But what about heresy? Some Christians take heresy to mean any point of disagreement with their tradition or way of thinking. But that's not how Christians have historically understood the word. "Heresy" literally means "choice" and refers to a willful deviation from orthodox teaching.[15] Heretics, then, deny a central truth or truths of the Christian faith.

But why all this fuss about orthodoxy? Why is it so important to Christianity? Ben Quash provides a helpful answer:

York Press, 2009);

[13]For a helpful discussion, see Paul Harris, *Elements of Pantheism: A Spirituality of Nature and the Universe,* 3rd edition (CreateSpace Independent Publishing, 2013), 35-47.

[14]Justin S. Holcomb, *Know the Heretics* (Grand Rapids, MI: Zondervan, 2014), 10.

[15]Ibid., 11.

But there is a very good and positive reason why Christianity has been so concerned about orthodoxy, or right belief. From its very beginnings, Christianity said that neither your race, nor your sex, nor your social class, nor your age could ever be a bar to full membership of Christ's body, the Church. Anyone could be a Christian: you didn't have to be born in the right place at the right time to the right parents. Christ's salvation was offered to you whether or not you were a Jew or a Gentile, slave or free person, a woman or a man. This was radical stuff. What, though, was left to mark a Christian out from a non-Christian? The answer was: your faith—what you believed in, as embodied in your practices and confessed with your lips.[16]

The Church's identity is tightly bound up with orthodox teaching, and that's why heresy is such a serious matter. As Quash rightly suggests, "It [heresy] threatened a crucial thing that bound the Church together and made Christians Christians."[17]

Finally, let us consider the difference between a cult and the occult. People often mistakenly equate the two. There's good reason for this. Sometimes cults participate in the occult, but not all do. The word "cult" in English is used in a variety of ways. Sometimes it's simply used in pop-culture when a certain personality, T.V. show, music group, or the like has a significant fan-base (e.g., the cult of Doctor Who). Sometimes people use the word cult to describe a religion that's different than their own. There is, however, a third and more nuanced understanding of a cult. Here we might speak of "religious cults" or "new religious movements." Some widely recognized religious cults include Heaven's Gate, Branch Davidians, and The People's Temple, all of which ended tragically with the death of their followers. Religious cults differ from denominations in a significant way, as Ed Hindson explains:

> Religious cults are schismatic deviations of established religious bodies. They are generally led by a powerful individual who is convinced that he or she has the only true message of God. The result is a bizarre system of deviant doctrine built upon the claim of extrabiblical revelation. Religious cults differ from denominations in that they are heretical schisms from orthodox beliefs and practices. Unlike Christian denominations, which differ from one another in doctrinal views and polity practices, cults exclude all other religious groups as false, and teach that they alone are going to heaven.[18]

Religious cults, especially those that deviate from orthodox Christianity, often share the following traits:

- Exclusivist in knowledge, believing their leader or group alone has found the truth others have missed or misunderstood.

---

[16]Ben Quash, "Prologue," in *Heresies and How to Avoid Them: Why It Matters What Christians Believe*, eds. Ben Quash and Michael Ward (Grand Rapids, MI: Baker Academic, 2009), 1.

[17]Ibid., 2.

[18]Ed Hindson, "Cults, Characteristics of," in *The Popular Encyclopedia of Apologetics: Surveying the Evidence for the Truth of Christianity*, ed. Ed Hindson and Ergun Caner (Eugene, OR; Harvest House Publishers, 2008), 158.

- Exclusivist regarding salvation, believing salvation comes only through their group's teaching and practices.

- Reliance on extrabiblical revelation, whether a sacred text (e.g., book of Mormon, New World Translation), visions, dreams, or prophecy.

- Denial of the Christian doctrine of the Trinity.

- Defective view of the person and work of Christ, especially denying Jesus' divinity and salvation through Him alone.[19]

The occult, on the other hand, places emphasis on gaining forbidden knowledge or power through supernatural means, "such as astrology, fortune telling, psychic, spiritism, Kabbalah, parapsychology, witchcraft, magick, paganism, and Satinism."[20] Those within a cult (or religion, such as Wicca) might practice the occult, but not all do.

False Teaching in the New Testament

Warnings against false teaching permeate the pages of the New Testament, especially in the New Testament letters. As we proceed, we'll see that the early church wrestled against a variety of false teachings, ranging from false beliefs on ethical behavior and practices, the second coming, Jesus's resurrection, the deity and humanity of Christ, Scripture, and the nature of the Gospel in relation to the law. Jesus, too, had quite a bit to say about false teachers, warning against them. Let's begin with Jesus' teachings, and then work our way through the rest of the New Testament letters.

Jesus on False Teaching

In Jesus' day, Judaism consisted of a variety of sects, but two stand out from the pages of Scripture—the Sadducees and the Pharisees. The Pharisees, who were the religious leaders of Israel, leaned toward a theological conservativism, though they also tended toward legalism and hypocrisy. On multiple occasions, Jesus exposed their hypocrisy. Take, for example, the following passage:

> [2] The scribes and the Pharisees sit on Moses' seat, [3] so do and observe whatever they tell you, but not the works they do. For they preach, but do not practice. [4] They tie up heavy burdens, hard to bear, and lay them on people's shoulders, but they themselves are not willing to move them with their finger. [5] They do all their deeds to be seen by others. For they make their phylacteries broad and their fringes long, [6] and they love the place of honor at feasts and the best seats in the synagogues [7] and greetings in the marketplaces and being called rabbi by others. (Mt 23:2-7)

---

[19]Ibid., 158-161.

[20]James Walker, "Occult," in *The Popular Encyclopedia of Apologetics: Surveying the Evidence for the Truth of Christianity*, ed. Ed Hindson and Ergun Caner (Eugene, OR, Harvest House Publishers, 2008), 367.

Again, in the same chapter, Jesus called out the Pharisees for traveling great distances to make converts; yet, in so doing, they made their converts "twice as much a child of hell" as they themselves were (v. 15). He likens them as "blind guides" leading the blind (v.16).

In another part of the passage, Jesus charges the Pharisees with nitpicking the finer points of the law, while neglecting "the weightier matters," such as "justice, mercy and faithfulness" (v. 23) They "clean the outside of the cup and the plate, but inside they are full of greed and self-indulgence" (v. 25). Jesus instructs them to be more concerned about what's going on inwardly than outwardly, for, as He put it in a different place, out of our hearts flow evil thoughts and actions, and that's what defiles the person (Mt 15:18-20)

The Sadducees, who were also religious leaders, and most likely aristocratic, denied certain teachings of Judaism accepted by the Pharisees, such as the resurrection from the dead, angels, and spirits (Mt 22:23; Acts 4:1-2; 23:8). On one occasion, the Sadducees started up a debate with Jesus, trying to trap him. According to Moses, they claim, if a man dies with no children, then his brother should marry his widow and raise up children on his behalf. But suppose that there were seven brothers, each of whom had married the widow and each of whom had died. At the resurrection, which of the seven brothers would be her husband? (Mt 22:23-28) Jesus stands their objection on its head.

> [29] But Jesus answered them, "You are wrong, because you know neither the Scriptures nor the power of God. [30] For in the resurrection they neither marry nor are given in marriage, but are like angels in heaven. [31] And as for the resurrection of the dead, have you not read what was said to you by God: [32] 'I am the God of Abraham, and the God of Isaac, and the God of Jacob'? He is not God of the dead, but of the living." (Mt 22:29-32)

Here, Jesus corrects several false doctrinal beliefs the Sadducees had. First, we see that Jesus corrected their view of God. They had a weak view of, what theologians call, God's omnipotence (divine power). Jesus suggests that divine omnipotence includes God's ability to raise the dead. Second, Jesus corrects their false view about the resurrection. The Sadducees denied the resurrection. To show their folly, Jesus appeals to those Scriptures—the Pentateuch (first five books of the Old Testament)—that the Sadducees accepted as authoritative. He appeals to God's own words, which declares that He's the God of Abraham, Isaac, and Jacob. Why is that significant? When God said this to Moses, Abraham, Isaac, and Jacob had all been dead for over four hundred years. But God is speaking in the present tense, indicating that, minimally, we can infer from this that there is an afterlife, and that the bodies of Abraham, Isaac, and Jacob are as good as raised. Christians have traditionally held to the belief that a person's immaterial part (whether one's soul or spirit) survives death and that eventually God will raise them bodily from the dead. One could argue that Jesus is teaching something very similar here, that is to say, Abraham, Isaac, and Jacob are alive in some sense, and that they'll one day be raised. Nevertheless, Jesus affirms the resurrection. Third, and lastly, Jesus affirms the existence of angels. Jesus suggests that in our resurrected state, we'll not be concerned with marriage, just as the angels in heaven are not concerned with it.

Not only did Jesus warn against the false teaching of the Pharisees and Sadducees, He also warned against coming false prophets. These false prophets "come to you in sheep's clothing but inwardly are ravenous wolves" (Mt 7:15). He goes on to say that we'll "recognize them by their fruits" (v. 16). In other words, we'll recognize them by their actions and what they say. Jesus even suggests that we'll encounter people claiming to be "the Christ." These false prophets perform great signs and miracles, but they ultimately seek to lead people astray (Mt 24:23-24). Lastly, Jesus reminds us that not everyone who calls Him Lord belongs to Him:

> [21] "Not everyone who says to me, 'Lord, Lord,' will enter the kingdom of heaven, but the one who does the will of my Father who is in heaven. [22] On that day many will say to me, 'Lord, Lord, did we not prophesy in your name, and cast out demons in your name, and do many mighty works in your name?' [23] And then will I declare to them, 'I never knew you; depart from me, you workers of lawlessness.'" (Mt 7:21-23)

Jesus recognized that just because a person claims to do something in His name, doesn't mean that he or she is His follower. This passage shows that we can't rely merely on people's outward actions to see whether they're genuine followers of Christ.

The Letters on False Teaching

The New Testament letters also warn against false teachings. The authors of 2 Peter, Jude, and 2 John all wrote with the intention of warning against false teaching. Consider the following passages:

> But false prophets also arose among the people, just as there will be false teachers among you, who will secretly bring in destructive heresies, even denying the Master who bought them, bringing upon themselves swift destruction. [2] And many will follow their sensuality, and because of them the way of truth will be blasphemed. [3] And in their greed they will exploit you with false words. (2 Peter 2:1-3)

> [4] For certain people have crept in unnoticed who long ago were designated for this condemnation, ungodly people, who pervert the grace of our God into sensuality and deny our only Master and Lord, Jesus Christ. (Jude 4)

There are several points to take away from these passages. First, false teachers often clandestinely creep into our churches. This echoes what Jesus taught about the false teachers coming as wolves in sheep's clothing. The Apostle Paul, too, uses this language to describe false teachers (Acts 20:29). Second, false teachers bring with them two things when they enter our churches: false teaching and false practices. False teachers deny central teachings of the Christian faith (e.g., denying Jesus or perverting God's grace), bringing with them "destructive heresies." They also live out sensuous lifestyles, using their words to deceive and "exploit" believers. Peter tells us they do this out of their "greed."

So far, we've only considered broadly a few examples of what the New Testament letters say about false teaching. In what follows, we're going to examine specific kinds of false teaching and false practices.

Syncretism, Angels, and Asceticism: Christianity arose out of Judaism, but quickly exploded throughout the Roman Empire. Many factors led to the expansion of the Christian movement, one of which was the missionary efforts of the apostle Paul. A large portion of the New Testament consists of letters Paul wrote as follow-up correspondences to the churches he founded during his missionary journeys. Much like the United States is today, the religious landscape of the Roman Empire was a melting pot of ideas and practices. Paul understood this and encouraged the churches in his letters to avoid syncretistic practices. Syncretism occurs when a person blends or merges into her worldview various religious beliefs, ideologies, and/or practices that are contradictory. We see this very practice of syncretism taking place in Colossae, where believers were falling prey to a heresy that blended elements from Judaism and paganism.

In his letter to the Colossians, Paul warns: "Be careful not to allow anyone to captivate you through an empty, deceitful philosophy that is according to human traditions and the elemental spirits of the world, and not according to Christ." (Col 2:8, NET Bible) As pointed out in a previous chapter, Paul's warning isn't against the use of philosophy; rather, he's more concerned that his readers aren't duped by philosophies grounded in merely human or worldly ways of thinking—the kinds of philosophies that aren't grounded in Christ, who, according to Paul, is the source of all wisdom and knowledge (Col 2:3). Christ is the embodiment of deity (Col 1:19; 2:9) and the wellspring of all knowledge and wisdom.

Paul outlines the core tenets of this "deceitful philosophy" in the following way:

> [16] Therefore let no one pass judgment on you in questions of food and drink, or with regard to a festival or a new moon or a Sabbath. [17] These are a shadow of the things to come, but the substance belongs to Christ. [18] Let no one disqualify you, insisting on asceticism and worship of angels, going on in detail about visions, puffed up without reason by his sensuous mind, [19] and not holding fast to the Head, from whom the whole body, nourished and knit together through its joints and ligaments, grows with a growth that is from God.

> [20] If with Christ you died to the elemental spirits of the world, why, as if you were still alive in the world, do you submit to regulations— [21] "Do not handle, Do not taste, Do not touch" [22] (referring to things that all perish as they are used)—according to human precepts and teachings? [23] These have indeed an appearance of wisdom in promoting self-made religion and asceticism and severity to the body, but they are of no value in stopping the indulgence of the flesh.

This false philosophy consisted of angel worship, asceticism, and following certain regulations of the Jewish law. Regarding angel worship, note Paul's use of the phrase: "elemental spirits of the world" (2:8, 20). There is debate on the exact meaning of "elemental spirits" or, as it could be translated, "basic principles." Richard Melick explains:

Here Paul used the term "basic principles" (*stoicheia*), which has a long history of interpretation. Originally, the term referred to the four basic elements of the world: earth, fire, wind, and water. These were often seen in conflict with each other. The term was later used of the basic elements of words, the alphabet. The construction of the alphabet allowed the formation of words and communication of ideas. The word later came to mean the "ABC's" of something, i.e., the basics. In some teachings, the "elements" were the signs of the zodiac and the powers that occupied the planets. These powers supposedly exerted their influence over the world and its activities. In Jewish circles, the term "elements" often applied to supernatural beings who ruled over people. Some considered them demons. Paul used the term in Gal 4:9, where he confronted false teachers who urged Christians to worship the elementary things. Paul opposed them as "no-gods," undeserving of worship. Even so, the Galatians were in danger of turning to them.[21]

More than likely, "elemental spirits" is a reference to supernatural or angelic beings thought to rule over the world.[22] This reading of the terminology makes sense, given Paul's insistence on the superiority of Christ over such beings (1:15-18; 2:15) and that the Colossians not give into angel worship (2:18). Furthermore, Colossians 2:15 uses the language of "rulers and authorities," which we also see mentioned in Ephesians 3:10, where Paul adds that they are "in the heavenly places."[23]

Regarding asceticism and the Jewish law, Paul recognized that such practices appear to have wisdom; however, they ultimately fail. Christ is the true source of wisdom, who is the head of the church. It is in him that we find nourishment and are built up together. Again, Christ is superior in all ways. Asceticism and the keeping of certain Jewish traditions will not bring about true holiness. Therefore, we should keep our faith looking to and grounded in Christ.

Resurrection, Second Coming, and the Gospel: Throughout his letters, Paul addressed several other false teachings. We're going to consider three, beginning with false teaching on the resurrection. In a second letter written to his young apprentice, Timothy, Paul warned about a pair of teachers, Hymenaeus and Philetus. These two men had "swerved from the truth" and were "upsetting the faith of some" (2 Tim 2:18). Apparently, these false teachers had been teaching that the resurrection had already taken place (v. 18).

On the other end of the spectrum, some in Corinth had denied that there was such a thing as a resurrection from the dead. But Paul has quite a bit to say about that too:

[12] Now if Christ is proclaimed as raised from the dead, how can some of you say that there is no resurrection of the dead? [13] But if there is no resurrection of the dead, then not even Christ has been raised. [14] And if Christ has not been raised, then our preaching is in vain and your faith is in vain. [15] We are even found to be

[21]Richard R. Melick, *Philippians, Colossians, Philemon*, vol. 32, The New American Commentary (Nashville, TN: Broadman and Holman Publishers, 1991), 253.
[22]Ibid.
[23]For further reading, see Michael S. Heiser, *The Unseen Realm: Recovering the Supernatural Worldview of the Bible* (Bellingham, WA: Lexham Press, 2015), 330.

misrepresenting God, because we testified about God that he raised Christ, whom he did not raise if it is true that the dead are not raised. [16] For if the dead are not raised, not even Christ has been raised. [17] And if Christ has not been raised, your faith is futile and you are still in your sins. [18] Then those also who have fallen asleep in Christ have perished. [19] If in Christ we have hope in this life only, we are of all people most to be pitied.

[20] But in fact Christ has been raised from the dead, the firstfruits of those who have fallen asleep (1 Cor 15:12-20)

In this passage, Paul makes it clear that there's an intricate connection between Jesus' resurrection and our own resurrection. His argument is subtle, and if we're not careful we'll miss it. Central to Jewish and Christian teaching is the resurrection of the dead. Note Paul doesn't say if Christ isn't raised then there's no resurrection of the dead; rather, he's arguing that if there is no resurrection from the dead, then not even Jesus has been raised. Through Modus Tollens, Paul argues:

P1: If there is no resurrection from the dead, then not even Christ has been raised

P2: But Christ has been raised from the dead

C: Therefore, there is a resurrection from the dead

Paul reiterates to his hearers that if there is no resurrection from the dead, and if Christ isn't raised, then our preaching is in vain and we're misrepresenting God. It is through the resurrection that Christ has defeated death, which will ultimately be destroyed (v. 26).

Paul makes two corrections to the false teaching on the resurrection. First, the resurrection is a central doctrine of the Christian faith, which is intricately connected to Christ's resurrection. Christ, the first fruits from the dead, defeated death, and it's because of this we can look forward to our own resurrected bodies. Second, the resurrection from the dead has not yet happened. Christ's resurrection is a foreshadowing of what is to come, when we, too, will be raised in his likeness (Phil 3:20-21; 1 Jn 3:2).

A second area Paul addresses is on the second coming. Just as Hymenaeus and Philetus falsely taught regarding the resurrection, some had been teaching the Thessalonians that the second coming had already taken places. Paul warns them "not to be quickly shaken in mind or alarmed, either by a spirit or spoken word, or a letter seeming to be from us, to the effect that the day of the Lord has come" (2 Thes 2:2). Paul assures his readers that the second coming is still yet to come and that a number of certain other events must first take place before Christ's return (2 Thes 2:3-12).

Paul also addresses a third area in his letters—the Gospel. At the center of the Gospel for Paul is the deity, death, and resurrection of Jesus (1 Cor 15:1-3; Gal 1:1-3). Stemming out from Christ's deity, death, and resurrection is the doctrine of salvation by God's grace through faith. Some in Galatia had been swayed to abandon the Gospel, which led to some sharp words from Paul:

> [6] I am astonished that you are so quickly deserting him who called you in the grace of Christ and are turning to a different gospel— [7] not that there is another one, but there are some who trouble you and want to distort the gospel of Christ. [8] But even if we or an angel from heaven should preach to you a gospel contrary to the one we preached to you, let him be accursed. (Gal 1:6-8)

False teachers, known as Judaizers, had been teaching that works of the law were necessary for salvation. Paul sharply rebukes this:

> [15] We ourselves are Jews by birth and not Gentile sinners; [16] yet we know that a person is not justified by works of the law but through faith in Jesus Christ, so we also have believed in Christ Jesus, in order to be justified by faith in Christ and not by works of the law, because by works of the law no one will be justified. (Gal 2:15-16)

In this passage (and others), Paul emphasizes that justification (i.e., God declaring a person righteous) comes through faith and not through the observation of the law. That's not to say that the law is bad. The law certainly has its place. The law condemns us, showing us what sin is, and like a tutor, leads us to Christ (Gal 3:19, 24). But life comes through the finished work of Christ and the empowering work of the Holy Spirit, which we receive through faith and not the law (Gal 2:19-21; 3:5).

Scripture and the Nature of Christ: Like Paul, Jesus' disciple John warned against false teaching in his letters. One area that concerned John was adding to or taking away from Scripture (Rev 22:18-19). We'll need to look at some additional passages to flesh out why this is so important.

Paul tells us that all Scripture is "breathed out by God" and is "profitable for teaching, for reproof, for correction, and for training in righteousness" (2 Tim 3:16). This passage teaches that it's the very words (the *graphē*) themselves that are "breathed out by God." In a similar manner, Peter reminds us that prophecy isn't a matter of a person's interpretation, nor is it produced through "the will of man"; rather, "men spoke from God as they were carried along by the Holy Spirit" (2 Pet 1:20-21). Though God used human authors to communicate to us, the Bible isn't merely a compilation of human writings, nor is it merely a human book— though it certainly contains a diversity of human conventions, such as a variety of writing styles among the authors, multiple genres (e.g., poetry, narrative, Gospels, letters, prophecy, apocalyptic, history, and wisdom literature) and sub-genres, figures of speech, and the like. The Scriptures, including all prophecy, is a product of God Himself. In other words, the Bible is the product of, what theologians call, "dual-authorship," with God as the primary author.

Given that Scripture is a product of dual-authorship, John's concern makes sense. Adding to or taking away from the Scriptures is adding to or taking away from what God says, and this goes against, what theologians call, "the Scripture Principle." In other words, the Bible doesn't contain the Word of God nor does it become the Word of God nor is it merely witness to the Word of God; rather, *the*

Bible is the Word of God. One of the oldest deceptions in human history stems from doubting God's Word. In Genesis 3 the serpent asks: "Has God said?" False teachers today ask this same question. John understood the dangers of adding to or taking away from God's Word, that is, what God has given to us through His self-revelation.

Another area of concern for John stems from false teaching on the nature of Christ. Most cults today deny either Jesus' humanity or His deity. This was also true in John's day. Let's look at what the Elder tells us about these false teachers.

> [18] Children, it is the last hour, and as you have heard that antichrist is coming, so now many antichrists have come. Therefore we know that it is the last hour. [19] They went out from us, but they were not of us; for if they had been of us, they would have continued with us. But they went out, that it might become plain that they all are not of us. [20] But you have been anointed by the Holy One, and you all have knowledge. [21] I write to you, not because you do not know the truth, but because you know it, and because no lie is of the truth. [22] Who is the liar but he who denies that Jesus is the Christ? This is the antichrist, he who denies the Father and the Son. [23] No one who denies the Son has the Father. Whoever confesses the Son has the Father also. [24] Let what you heard from the beginning abide in you. If what you heard from the beginning abides in you, then you too will abide in the Son and in the Father. [25] And this is the promise that he made to us—eternal life.

> [26] I write these things to you about those who are trying to deceive you. [27] But the anointing that you received from him abides in you, and you have no need that anyone should teach you. But as his anointing teaches you about everything, and is true, and is no lie—just as it has taught you, abide in him.

We can learn several things about these false teachers from this passage. First, the Elder tells us that these false teachers "went out from us." However, though they came from him and the other apostles, they're not of them. Why is that? Because they've changed the message. They've denied something significant about Jesus. Second, He calls such false teachers "the antichrist." When people hear the word "antichrist," they have in mind the malevolent world leader during the tribulation. In this passage, the antichrist is someone who's denied that "Jesus is the Christ." In denying that Jesus is the Son of God is to deny the Father. Third, we see that these false teachers "are trying to deceive" those to whom he's writing. John affirms that those who confess Jesus (the Son) have the Father, and if they "abide" in what they've heard from the beginning, they are abiding "in the Son and in the Father." These false teachers, on the other hand, rejected that Jesus is the Christ, the anointed Messiah, who was sent from God. In rejecting Christ, they also reject the Father.

We see this word "antichrist" in two other passages from John's epistles (letters). First, we see it in 1 John 4:3, where the Elder tells us that "every spirit that does not confess Jesus is not from God." The second passage is 2 John 7. In this passage, the Elder tells us that "many deceivers have gone out into the world," and that anyone who does "not confess the coming of Jesus in the flesh" is the antichrist. In other words, those who do not confess Jesus as the Son of God or who deny Jesus came in the flesh are deceivers and the antichrist. They are against

Christ! By denying Jesus, these individuals also deny the Father. What a person does with Jesus becomes the litmus test for fellowship among our Christian communities.

False Teaching in the Early Church

Having taken quite a bit of space discussing false teaching in the New Testament, let's turn to some common heresies the early Church wrestled against. We'll begin by examining certain Christological heresies, that is, heresies that deny either Jesus' deity or His humanity. Following those, we'll consider two Trinitarian heresies. These differ from Christological heresies in that they deny either the unity or distinctiveness of the persons of the Trinity.

Christological Heresies

In modern times, many of the doctrinal discussions that take place within the church revolve around salvation, end times, church polity, cultural issues, and the like. Among the earliest Christians, Christology remained front and center, standing at the heart of the earliest controversies. This makes sense. Christianity came out of Judaism, which is a monotheistic religion. Monotheism is the view that only one all-powerful, creator God exists. In Jewish monotheistic thinking, several beliefs set the God of Israel apart from the gods of the nations. Richard Bauckham names the following:

- God is the sole Creator of all things (all others are created by God)

- God is the sole sovereign Ruler over all things (all others are subject to God's rule)

- God will achieve his eschatological rule (when all creatures acknowledge YHWH's sole deity)

- The name YHWH names God in his unique identity

- God alone may and must be worshiped (since worship is acknowledgement of God's sole deity)

- God alone is fully eternal (self-existent from past to future eternity)[24]

Coming out of such a Jewish context, how is it, then, that these early Christians, on the one hand, held firmly to monotheism, and yet, on the other, worshiped Jesus? How could Jesus be God, if there's only one God? How could Jesus be both human and divine? This was *the* struggle of the early Church. They sought

---

[24]Richard Bauckham, *Jesus and the God of Israel: God Crucified and Other Studies on the New Testament's Christology of Divine Identity* (Grand Rapids, MI: Wm B. Eerdmans Publishing Co., 2009), 234.

to be faithful to the Scriptures; yet, they also sought to translate the ideas and concepts found in Scripture into their own cultural contexts, using familiar ideas and terminology. This struggle resulted in the production of several Christological heresies—heresies that either denied one of the two natures of Christ or denied the unity of the two natures. We'll briefly consider seven:

> **Ebionism**: Perhaps the oldest Christological heresy, this view denied Jesus' divinity and was most likely Jewish in origin. Ebionites insisted upon observance of the law. Some held to Jesus' supernatural birth, while others did not. All rejected Christ's preexistence and believed He was just a man.

> **Docetism**: Docetism comes from the Greek word *dokein*, which means "to seem." Rather than denying Jesus' divinity, this view suggested that it only seemed Jesus came in human flesh. This view was most likely influenced by Gnosticism, which stressed that ultimate redemption comes through knowledge. Gnostics believed material things were evil, which would explain why Docetists rejected Jesus coming in the flesh. Given its early nature, this Christological heresy could very well have been the false teaching mentioned in 1 John.

> **Dynamic Monarchianism**: This view, espoused by Theoditus (c. AD 190) and Paul of Samosata (c. AD 260), denied Jesus' divinity. It placed primary emphasis on the Father, suggesting that God came upon or adopted Jesus, who was a supremely virtuous man.

> **Arianism**: This view derived from the teachings of Arius (c. AD 250-336). The Son is neither uncreated nor eternal nor of the same substance as the Father; rather, the Son is the first and highest over all of God's creatures and is of a similar substance as the Father (*homoiousius*). The word "Son" served more as an honorific term. Arianism denies the divinity of Jesus.

> **Apollinarianism**: Based on the thought of Apollinarius (c. AD 31-390), this view denied Christ's full humanity. Instead of having a rational soul and body, the Word took the place of the soul, uniting to the body of Christ. Apollinarius believed that Christ had only one nature, instead of two (both human and divine).

> **Nestorianism**: This Christological heresy developed out of a controversy between Nestorius (AD 386-451), the patriarch of Constantinople, and Cyril of Alexandria (AD 378-444) over the use of the word *theotokos* ("the mother of God"). Cyril accused Nestorius (some believe wrongly) of advocating that there was a division between the humanity and divinity of Christ, which would later result in the "two-persons" view of Christ.

> **Eutychianism**: Eutyches (c. AD 375-454) suggested that before the incarnation, Christ had two natures, but subsequently, the two natures morphed into one divine/human hybrid nature.[25]

---

[25]Millard J. Erickson, *The Word Became Flesh: A Contemporary Incarnational Christology* (Grand Rapids, MI: Baker Books, 1991), 41-64.

After years of wading through such Christological controversies, the early Church formulated two main creedal formulas, hammering out what they took to be a biblically faithful representation of, on the one hand, Jesus' relationship to the Father and Spirt, and, on the other, His divinity and humanity. The first was a polemic against Arianism. Established in June of AD 325, the Nicene Creed places focus on Jesus' relationship with the Father.

Nicene Creed

We believe in one God, the Father, the almighty [pantokratōr], the maker of all things seen and unseen.

And in one Lord Jesus Christ, the Son of God; begotten from the Father; only-begotten—that is, form the substance from the Father; God from God; light from light; true God from true God; begotten not made; being of one substance with the Father [homoousion tō patri]; through whom all things in heaven and on earth came into being; who on account of us human beings and our salvation came down and took flesh, becoming a human being [sarkōthenta, enanthrōpōsanta]; he suffered and rose again on the third day, ascended into the heavens; and will come again to judge the living and the dead.

And in the Holy spirit.

As for those who say that "there was when he was not," and "before being born he was not," and "he came into existence out of nothing," or who declare that the Son of God is of a different substance or nature, or is subject to alteration or change—the catholic and apostolic church condemns these.[26]

The debate centered on whether Jesus was of a similar substance as the Father (*homoiousion tō patri*) or whether He was of the same substance (*homoousion tō patri*). The council sided with those claiming that the Father and Son were of the *same substance*. It all hung on a single *iota*![27] Not only did the Creed of Nicaea affirm that Jesus is of the same substance as the Father, it reaffirmed the biblical teaching on the Son's preexistence and eternality.

The second formula, the Chalcedonian Creed (AD 451), which built on all that Nicaea established, set in motion certain parameters for thinking about the divinity and humanity of Christ.

Chalcedonian Creed

Following the holy Fathers, we all with one voice confess our Lord Jesus Christ to be one and the same Son, perfect in divinity and humanity, truly God and truly human, consisting of a rational soul and body, being of one substance with the Father in relation to his divinity, and being of one substance with us in relation to his humanity, and is like us in all things apart from sin (Hebrews 4:15). He was begotten

---

[26]"The Nicene Creed," in *The Christian Theology Reader*, 4th ed., edited by Alister E. McGrath (Malden, ME: Wiley-Blackwell, 2011), 9.

[27]An *iota* is a Greek letter of the alphabet that resembles the English letter "i".

of the Father before time in relation to his divinity, and in these recent days, was born from the Virgin Mary, the Theotokos, for us and for our salvation. In relation to the humanity, he is one and the same Christ, the Son, the Lord, the only begotten, who is to be acknowledged in two natures, without confusion, without change, without division, and without separation. This distinction of natures is in no way abolished an account of this union, but rather the characteristic property of each nature is preserved, and concurring into one Person and one subsistence, not as if Christ were parted or divided into two persons, but remains one and the same Son and only-begotten God, Word, Lord, Jesus Christ; even as the Prophets from the beginning spoke concerning him, and our Lord Jesus Christ instructed us, and the Creed of the Fathers was handed down to us.[28]

Rather than giving a full-on definition of Christ, the Chalcedonian statement provides certain parameters for thinking about the unity between the divinity and humanity of Christ. Much like guardrails, these parameters keep Christians within the acceptable lines of orthodoxy. The following line is central to the Creed's main thrust, that Christ is "to be acknowledged in two natures, without confusion, without change, without division, and without separation." Theologians refer to this unity between the two natures as the *hypostatic union*. In becoming flesh (Jn 1:14), the eternal Word of God added to Himself a human nature; yet, the two natures remain what they are essentially. There's no blending or morphing between the two natures, nor are the natures diminished, divisible, or separated. The early Church understood that it was necessary for the Son of God to take on our humanity, that is, to become like us in every way, yet without sin, and in so doing it was for our salvation. As Athanasius said long ago, "it was our sorry case that caused the Word to come down."[29]

Trinitarian Heresies

Having briefly examined Christological heresies, now shall we turn to two major Trinitarian heresies: modalism and tri-theism. Before examining each, it may help to take a quick refresher on the classical Christian doctrine of the Trinity.

Perhaps, there's no doctrine that sets Christianity apart from other theisms more than that of the Trinity. Like other theistic views, Christians believe there is only one God—a view known as monotheism. Monotheists believe that God is personal; however, there are differences among monotheists on how to understand God's personhood. Jews and Muslims, and most other non-Christian monotheists, are Unitarian. In other words, they believe God consists of only one singular divine person. Christians, on the other hand, are Trinitarian, meaning they believe that God consists of three divine persons—Father, Son, and Holy Spirit—in one substance or essence. Each divine Persons is distinct from the others, though without separation. The Father is not the Son or Spirit, the Son is not

---

[28]"The Chalcedonian Definition of the Christian Faith (451)," in *The Christian Theology Reader*, 4th ed., edited by Alister E. McGrath (Malden, ME: Wiley-Blackwell, 2011), 238.

[29] Athanasius, *On the Incarnation*, 1.2.

the Father or the Spirit, and the Spirit is not the Son or Father. Yet, each person is divine. The Father is God, the Son is God, and the Holy Spirit is God. Each of the persons are co-equal in power and co-eternal.

In working out an understanding of the doctrine of the Trinity, the early church sought to preserve two features of the Christian understanding of God—the unity and distinction of the divine persons. Trinitarian heresies generally overemphasize one or the other. Let's consider each in turn, beginning with modalism.

Modalism: At some point in your life, you may have heard someone compare God to H_2O. Just as water has three forms (depending on its temperature), God too has three forms, they say. At one point, water can be a liquid, it can also exist as a solid or as a gas. The same is true with God. At one moment God is Father, at another He is the Son, and, yet, at another, the Spirit. It's as if God morphs from one person to a different person, depending on the role He's playing in the economy of salvation. While modalism preserves God's unity, it obliterates the distinctiveness of persons within God.

Tritheism: In contrast to modalism, tritheism preserves the distinctiveness of the divine persons, but misses the mark on the unity. Generally, tritheists use language of God existing as three beings or as having three separate natures. As apologist Norman Geisler rightly suggests, "Few, if any, have held this view consciously, though unwittingly many have fallen into it verbally by their incautious language about the Godhead."[30] This is often true when talking to students about the Trinity. Without realizing it, they slip into tritheistic language. I find myself reminding them that distinction does not imply separation. The persons are distinct, but not separate from one another.

False Teaching Today

Having worked through false teaching within the New Testament and early church, let us conclude this chapter by outlining several non-Christian ideologies and worldviews that have permeated our culture. Given space restraints, we cannot go into each of these "isms" and worldviews in detail. My hope is only to give a very brief snapshot of some dangerous and destructive philosophies Christians often encounter.

Agnosticism – The belief that one cannot know with certainty concerning God and reality.

Atheism – The belief that no god or gods exist.

Animism – the belief that spirits reside in all things within the universe

Deism – God created the world but cannot or chooses not to act in it.

---

[30]Norman L. Geisler, *Systematic Theology: God and Creation*, vol. 2 (Minneapolis, MN: Bethany House Publishers, 2003), 295.

Dualism – the view that two co-eternal, co-existent beings oppose one another (e.g., God and Satan).

Determinism/Fatalism – all events are ultimately decided by a supernatural force (e.g., God) or by physical means (e.g., the universe, psychology, or biology).

Ethnocentrism – the belief that one ethnic group is superior to all others

Existentialism – human existence, and hence meaning and purpose, is constituted by human choice.

Gnosticism – the belief that the material universe is evil and that one must obtain salvation through special knowledge.

Humanism – humans alone are the final authority for truth and meaning in the universe.

Hedonism – the idea that a person should live for pleasure in this life, without the thought of eternal consequence or reward.

Henotheism – the belief in many gods, but only one reigns supreme over the others.

Individualism – a view that places emphasis on individual freedom over the needs of the community or larger society.

Materialism – a person's ultimate concern is in gaining or having possessions

Monism – reality is made up of only one ultimate substance.

Moral Relativism – moral truths or judgments are relative with respect to a person's individual or societal perspective.

Narcissism – excessive self-centeredness or extreme selfishness, especially with respect to one's self-interest or appearance.

Nihilism – the recognition that all is, essentially, meaningless, thereby rejecting all religious beliefs or religious principles.

Panentheism – God is in the world or the world is in God, and though God in some sense needs the world, God transcends the world as a soul transcends the body.

Pluralism – the belief that reality is made up of many 'things' or that more than one view or philosophy is true.

Polytheism – a plurality of gods exists in the world.

Pragmatism – the view that suggests truth is based on whatever works for the individual or society.

Relativism – The belief that there are no objective or universal truths in the world.

Religious Pluralism – The belief that one or more religious belief/worldview is equally valid, accepted, or true.

Scientism – Science is the only means by which we come to know things in the world.

Secularism – The belief that there is no need for God in society for moral living and ethics.

Spiritualism – a non-dogmatic stance centered on emotional experience (feelings) rather than creeds, doctrines, or structured religion.

Sadly, much like the Christians in Colossae, modern Christians, too, fall into syncretistic practices, having absorbed some of these ideologies into their own thinking. That's why the apostle Paul warns: "See to it that no one takes you captive by philosophy and empty deceit, according to human tradition, according to the elemental spirits of the world, and not according to Christ" (Col. 2:8). As Christians, we must continually be aware of those philosophies that are grounded in human tradition and not in Christ. We must examine our own beliefs and see if what we believe remains in tune with the words of Scripture. The Elder John's words remain true for us today: "Beloved, do not believe every spirit, but test the spirits to see whether they are from God, for many false prophets have gone out into the world" (1 Jn 4:1).

Theology and Correct Doctrine

Throughout this chapter, we've tackled quite a bit, and we've only begun to scratch the surface. Hopefully, you've seen that the Bible, and hence Christianity, takes seriously right doctrine. It's vital to who we are as Christians. No wonder James, the brother of Jesus, warns against seeking to become teachers within the church (Js 3:1). Teaching requires handling God's Word accurately. As we conclude this chapter, may we see the value of theology in helping us to think rightly, guarding our hearts and minds against false teaching and false living.

Chapter Five

Removing Doubt

No Room for Doubt?

If you're like me, you grew up in an environment where it was considered wrong or sinful to doubt your faith. Perhaps you've heard someone say:

"Real Christians never doubt"

or

"People who doubt have a weak faith"

For those of us who have wrestled with doubt, we know that it can be a painful experience. Statements like those above only add salt to an already infected wound. But are these statements true? Let's consider each in order:

"Real Christians Never Doubt"

Is it true that real Christians never doubt? Before answering that question, it's important for us to consider why some people believe this. On this point, Gary Habermas is surely right in suggesting that those who make such statements often do so because they see doubt as the opposite of faith.[1] The problem with such an objection comes down to an improper definition of doubt. Habermas defines religious doubt "as the lack of certainty about the truthfulness of Christianity, one's own faith, or how it applies to real life situations."[2] This definition is helpful. It helps us to see that doubt is related to uncertainty of elements within one's faith. But as Habermas reminds us, uncertainty, though it affects our faith, isn't the opposite of faith.[3] Os Guinness agrees. For Guinness, doubt isn't the opposite of faith, nor is it unbelief. Regarding this crucial difference, he says:

---

[1]Gary R. Habermas, *Dealing with Doubt* (Chicago, IL: Moody Press, 1990), 14.

[2]Gary R. Habermas, *The Thomas Factor* (Nashville, TN: Broadman and Holman Publishers, 1999), 5.

[3]Habermas, *Dealing with Doubt*, 14.

The Bible makes a definite distinction between them [doubt and unbelief], though the distinction is not hard and fast. The word *unbelief* is usually used of a willful refusal to believe or of a deliberate decision to disobey. So, while doubt is a state of suspension between faith and unbelief, unbelief is a state of the mind that is closed against God, an attitude of heart that disobeys God as much as it disbelieves the truth. Unbelief is the consequent of settled choice. Since it is deliberate response to God's truth, unbelief is definitely held to be responsible.[4]

Guinness thusly likens doubt to having a "divided heart."[5] Lastly, Alister Mc-Grath reminds us that doubt isn't the same as skepticism, which he defines as "the decision to doubt everything deliberately, as a matter of principle."[6] People who struggle with doubt often do so unintentionally, but it's a real existential struggle. As we think about doubt, then, we must avoid thinking of it as it being the unbelief, skepticism, or the opposite of faith. Rather, we must understand doubt as a vicious struggle that's often painful. It's an issue of a divided heart and uncertainty.

Another reason some people think real Christians never doubt flows from the belief that people who doubt have a weak faith. As we answer the "weak faith" objection below, we'll see that some of the greatest heroes in the Bible struggled with doubt. Despite their doubt, they went on to achieve great things for God's kingdom.

The truth of the matter is most (probably all, though some will deny it) Christians struggle with doubt. This was true for me as a young Christian, wrestling with whether I was truly saved. Over the years, I've met many other Christians, too, who have struggled with this very same issue. Christians struggle with all sorts of questions about their faith. Consider the following:

Does God exist? If so, what kind of God exists?

Is the Bible the Word of God or is made up?

Why should we believe Christianity is true?

How could God ever love or forgive me?

If God is good and powerful, why does He allow all this evil in the world?

These kinds of questions plague and vex believer and unbeliever alike, weighing on us heavily. So, why is it that people doubt, especially believers?

Off hand, I can think of two reasons. First, we are finite creatures. As discussed in the chapter one, our knowledge is limited. We are not omniscient, and that's one of many qualities that sets us apart from God—the infinite, all-knowing, Creator. If you recall, that's the Creator/creature distinction. Not knowing every-

---

[4]Os Guinness, *God in the Dark: The Assurance of Faith Beyond a Shadow of Doubt* (Wheaton, IL: Crossway, 1996), 26.

[5]Ibid., 23.

[6]Alister McGrath, *Doubting: Growing Through the Uncertainties of Faith* (Downers Grove, IL: InterVarsity Press, 2006), 13.

thing keeps us humble, reminding us of our place in the created order. Our not knowing things keeps us inquisitive. So, some doubts generate from our ignorance of certain things. Second, though doubt isn't necessarily sinful, sometimes it comes about because of our sinfulness. As Paul stresses, we know the truth (e.g., about God), yet, we suppress it through our sinfulness (Rom 1:18). Yielding to sin in our lives has a way of keeping us from truth (Is 59:2). In his letter to the Ephesians, Paul described such people as walking "in the futility of their minds," and then goes on to say, "[t]hey are darkened in their understanding, alienated from the life of God because of their ignorance that is in them, due to their hardness of heart" (Eph 4:18). Such a way of living stands in stark contrast to new life that comes from God. Rather, we should "put off" our old selves and "be renewed in the spirit" of our minds, putting "on the new self" that has been "created after the likeness of God in true righteousness and holiness" (Eph 4:21-24).

Habermas provides yet a third possibility—spiritual warfare. Working from C. S. Lewis' famous *Screwtape Letters*, he reminds us of two extremes people generally take when it comes to the supernatural. Either Satan and demons are just myth or they stand behind every problem that plagues us. We must avoid either extreme and recognize that the Bible has quite a bit to say about the work of our spiritual enemies. As Habermas says, "the more balanced biblical position is to recognize the influence of demonic forces as a major factor (Eph. 6:10-18) and to deal with them accordingly."[7]

So far, we've considered three reasons standing behind doubt, but there are many more potential triggers. Take the following: genuine intellectual inquiry, syncretism of ideologies, psychological or medical causes, faulty view of God, trauma, poor health and lack of sleep, hypocrisy in the Church, anxiety over forgiveness of sin, and worry about the future.[8] We could easily take the rest of the chapter and deal with each of these; however, for our purposes, we're only going to consider a few of these below.

"Doubters Have Weak Faith"

So, what of the second objection? No doubt (pun intended) people wrestle with uncertainty in their faith, but does that mean their faith is weak? Not necessarily! The Bible is replete with examples of people who doubted. Job, Abraham and Sarah, Moses, Gideon, David, Elijah, Jonah, Jeremiah, John the Baptist, Peter, Thomas, and Paul all had their bouts with doubt. Granted, some did not recover well (e.g., Jonah), but others, however, went on to do great things for God's kingdom.

Consider Thomas. Upon hearing the news of Jesus' resurrection, he doubted, exclaiming: "Unless I see in his hands the mark of the nails, and place my finger into the mark of the nails, and place my hand into his side, I will never believe" (Jn 20:25). But eight days later, when confronted by the risen Lord, Thomas ex-

---

[7]Habermas, *Dealing with Doubt*, 24.
[8]Ibid., 25-35.

claimed "My Lord and my God!" (Jn 20:28) Though Thomas initially doubted, he was confronted by the evidence and believed. Church tradition tells us that Thomas traveled all the way to India, where he was later martyred for his faith. When met by the evidence, Thomas moved from uncertainty to certitude, so much so that he was willing to die for what he believed. Peter, too, wavered in his faith. Here's a guy who spent over three years with Jesus, but during Jesus' trial (Mk 14:66-72) he denied that he even knew Jesus—a flat-out lie! Not too long before that he declared Jesus as "the Christ, the Son of the living God" (Mt 16:16). What happened? Doubt! Peter's doubt led him to a place of fear, confusion, and ultimately denying the Lord. But like Thomas, after Jesus' resurrection and confrontation with the risen Lord, Peter became a prominent leader in the church and outspoken witness for Christ (Acts 2:14-36; Acts 3-4:31). He, too, according to church history, was martyred for his faith. Finally, consider John the Baptist. John was in prison for speaking out against King Herod's adultery. He had heard about Jesus' ministry, but wanted to make sure that He was the one who was to come—the Messiah. So, he sent his disciples to investigate. When asked whether he was the Messiah or not, Jesus responded: "Go and tell John what you hear and see: ⁵ the blind receive their sight and the lame walk, lepers are cleansed and the deaf hear, and the dead are raised up, and the poor have good news preached to them. ⁶ And blessed is the one who is not offended by me" (Mt 11:4-6). As John's disciples were leaving, Jesus asked the crowd: "What did you go out into the wilderness to see? A reed shaken by the wind?" (Mt 11:7) The obvious answer is "no." Jesus reminds them that what they went out to see was a prophet. On the one hand, Jesus' words are a sharp rebuke to John's doubt. But notice what he says next, "Truly, I say to you, among those born of women there has arisen no one greater than John the Baptist. Yet the one who is least in the kingdom of heaven is greater than he" (Mt 11:11). God used each of these men, despite their doubt and uncertainty.

One can also find examples of saints throughout church history, as well as modern "giants of the faith," who have struggled with doubt. The fourth century Church Father, Augustine (354-430), spent his life in pursuit of truth. Reared as a Christian by his mother, Monica, he later rebelled, dabbling in Manicheism and worldly pursuits. Through a series of events and painful struggles, Augustine later embraced his childhood faith at the age of 31. He eventually became a bishop and wrote many works impacting Christian thought immensely. Martin Luther (1483-1546), champion of the Protestant Reformation, wrestled with doubt about God's character, his calling, and salvation. In modern times, C. S. Lewis (1898-1963), the author of *Narnia* and *Mere Christianity*, struggled with immense pain over the death of his wife, which is recounted in *A Greif Observed*. Mother Teresa (1910-1997), who served selflessly the poor and orphans of Calcutta, wrestled with what seemed to be God's absence in her life.⁹ Prominent Christian philosopher, Nicholas Wolterstorff, struggled with doubt brought on by suffering. He wrote a mov-

⁹Mother Teresa and Brian Kolodiejchuk, *Mother Teresa: Come Be My Light: The Private Writings of the "Saint of Calcutta"* (Waterville, ME: Wheeler Publishing, 2008).

ing lament, documenting his own struggles over the death of his son, Eric, who died in a rock-climbing accident.[10] Other influential Christians who have openly struggled with doubt include:

William Alston (philosopher)

Mike Licona (apologist)

John Ortberg (author and pastor)

Philip Yancey (author).[11]

So, what's the moral of the story? Even the strongest among us doubt! I don't mean to claim that everyone who wrestles with their faith overcomes. Sadly, some do leave the faith because of doubt. Famous agnostic New Testament scholar, Bart Ehrman, is one among many.[12] But earnestly wrestling through doubt doesn't mean that you'll end up like Ehrman. We can be encouraged because we have, to borrow a phrase from the book of Hebrews, "a great cloud of witnesses" who have gone before us and who have come through on the other side of doubt. I've found in my own life, rather than dismantling my faith, a healthy dose of doubt deepened it. The same is true for many others who have wrestled with doubt. On this point, Habermas gives some sage advice:

> Believers like Job, Abraham, and Paul grew during their times of doubt, even when their faith underwent the harshest attacks. Today, too, while uncertainty can have negative results to be avoided, it can also help us to learn some indispensable lessons. Perhaps the main issue here is what Christians do about their struggles. To whom do we turn, and what is our attitude toward what is happening? What applications do we make?[13]

We must keep two things before us as we engage our doubts. First, we can be encouraged that we can grow from our sessions with doubt, pain, and suffering. Second, combating doubt takes work on our part, and it requires a certain level of intentionality.

---

[10]Nicholas Wolterstorff, *Lament for a Son* (Grand Rapids, MI: Wm B. Eerdmans Publishing Co., 2001).

[11]See William Alston, "A Philosopher's Way Back to Faith," in *God and the Philosophers: The Reconciliation of Faith and Reason*, ed. Thomas V. Morris (Oxford University Press, 1996), 19-31; Michael R. Licona, "I'm A Doubting Thomas," https://www.risenjesus.com/im-doubting-thomas, July 18, 2014; John Ortberg, *Faith and Doubt* (Grand Rapids, MI: Zondervan, 2008); Philip Yancey, *Where is God When It Hurts* (Grand Rapids, MI: Zondervan, 2002); and *Disappointment with God: Three Questions No One Asks Aloud* (Grand Rapids, MI: Zondervan, 1997); https://philipyancey.com/q-and-a-topics/faith-and-doubt.

[12]Bart D. Erhman, *God's Problem: How the Bible Fails to Answer Our Most Important Questions—Why We Suffer* (New York: HaperOne, 2008).

[13]Habermas, *The Thomas Factor*, 21.

Combating Doubt

How then should Christians combat doubt in their lives? As noted earlier, the thrust of this chapter deals with religious doubt. Let me say up front that I am not a psychiatrist, psychologist, counselor, or licensed professional. I'm a theologian. My skill set is limited. What I offer to you comes from my own experience, Scripture, and literature on religious doubt. Doubt is often multi-dimensional, and sometimes certain biological and psychological triggers are at work. If you're having doubt related to depression or an anxiety disorder, or thoughts of suicide, let me be as clear as possible—please seek professional help. There are many good Christian professionals who have been well trained, especially in the areas of anxiety and depression. Feel no shame in seeking help.

Fact-based Doubt

Having made the above disclaimer, a crucial first step in combating doubt comes in recognizing the kind of doubt experienced. As noted earlier, various triggers bring on doubt, leading to one of two basic kinds of doubt: (1) fact-based doubt and (2) emotion-based doubt.[14] Let's begin with fact-based doubt.

Fact-based doubt revolves around _____? You guessed it—facts! Those struggling with fact-based doubt generally have intellectual itches in need of scratching. Something might seem puzzling to them or they run up against a seemingly logical contradiction. For example, how is it that Christians believe, on the one hand, that only one God exists, yet, on the other, God is three persons? Doesn't that seem to be a logical contradiction? [15] Or, perhaps you've wrestled with the following objection from the problem of evil:

God is all-powerful

God is all-good

Evil exists

At face-value, these three statements taken together seem contradictory.[16]

---

[14]Those writing on doubt use differing taxonomies of doubt. Gary Habermas lists three major kinds of doubt: factual, emotional, and volitional. Os Guinness offers seven families of doubt: (1) doubt from ingratitude; (2) doubt from a faulty view of God; (3) doubt from weak foundations; (4) doubt from lack of commitment; (5) doubt from lack of growth; (6) doubt from unruly emotions; and (7) doubt from hidden conflicts. (See Habermas, *Dealing with Doubt*, 25-37; *The Thomas Factor*, 37-58; and Guinness, *God in the Dark*, 39-161.) For our purposes, we're only going to focus only on two species of doubt: fact-based and emotion-based. For those interested, I highly recommend Habermas' chapter on volitional doubt, which you can read at http://www.garyhabermas.com/books/dealing_with_doubt/dealing_with_doubt.htm.

[15]For a fuller discussion on this issue, see chapter four.

[16]Given space restrictions, we cannot tackle this here. Though rigorous, I highly recommend Alvin Plantinga, *God, Freedom, and Evil* (Grand Rapids, MI: Wm B. Eerdmans Publish-

Those wrestling with fact-based doubt want to know why something is the case. Pat answers just won't do. They're interested in facts, data, and good arguments. Recall Thomas. Once confronted by the evidence of the risen Lord, he believed and his doubt dissolved.

Sometimes finding the answer involves a lot of digging and searching. Gregory Boyd, in his book, *Benefit of the Doubt*, shares his experience of dealing with doubt. Much like a house of cards, he had built his belief system in such a way that if one of his beliefs were removed, the whole house would come down.

> Not surprisingly, as I continued to study and my worldview continued to expand, it was just a matter of time before a card in my rebuilt house got knocked out, bringing my house to the ground once again. Because I had been through this once before, this collapse wasn't nearly as devastating as my first crash, but it was nevertheless painful. I soon managed to reassemble my remaining theological cards and rebuild a still smaller, and therefore less vulnerable, house. But as I continued to study and grow, it was just a matter of time before the same thing happened again . . . and again.[17]

This cycle of building and rebuilding occurred a dozen times or so. Though Boyd never lost his faith, he realized that there was something fundamentally flawed in the way he was doing theology. He had built his faith on something other than the center, which is Christ. He had built his foundation on the inspiration and inerrancy of Scripture. But what if Scripture has errors? Would that mean we should throw the whole thing out? He, like many other Christians, believed Jesus because he believed the Scriptures to be inspired. His paradigm shift came when he realized that that he had the order reversed. He came to believe that the Bible was inspired because Jesus was God incarnate. He recalls,

> From years of researching and wrestling with this material, I discovered I have compelling reasons for believing that Jesus is the incarnation of God that *have nothing to do with the belief in the inspiration of Scripture*. Some of my reasons are *philosophical* in nature. For example, I find the biblical worldview that is centered on a Creator who has the loving character that Jesus reveals makes better sense of my total experience of the world than any competing story or theory. Some of my reasons are *existential* in nature. For example, the story of God of unsurpassable love who went to the furthest extreme possible to save a race of hopeless rebels "rings true" in the deepest part of my being. It is, in the words of C. S. Lewis, the greatest myth ever told, though unlike all other myths, this one gives us reason to believe it actually happened! And some of my reasons are more *spiritual* in nature. For example, I have on occasions experienced Christ in ways that would make it extremely hard for me to deny his reality.

> Yet, the most compelling and most objective reasons I have for believing in Christ are *historical* in nature.[18]

---

ing Co., 1974). Because of Plantinga's work, even most atheists now recognize that the logical problem from evil fails and that there is no logical contradiction between those beliefs.

[17]Gregory A. Boyd, *Benefit of the Doubt: Breaking the Idol of Certainty* (Grand Rapids, MI: Baker Books, 2013), 158-159.

[18]Ibid., 160.

Throughout the chapter, Boyd goes on to lay out several reasons historically for thinking that Jesus was the Son of God incarnate.[19] He learned that by placing Jesus at the center of his faith, he gained assurance for the inspiration and authority of Scripture.

Boyd is not alone in using this method. Apologist Gary Habermas takes a similar approach in his book *The Risen Jesus and Future Hope*.[20] Habermas makes a distinction between umbrella approaches (reliability of Scripture arguments) and "minimal facts" arguments (bottom up approaches). He recognizes that, if done carefully, good arguments can be made for the reliability and trustworthiness of Scripture, which move to the truthfulness of the major tenets of Christianity. There is, however, a major setback with reliability approaches: "Just because a work is generally trustworthy, it does not always follow that everything in it (and especially the supernatural) is true."[21] Habermas prefers the minimal facts approach, which he developed through his own struggle with doubt. The minimal facts approach accepts only those facts allowed by critical New Testament scholars across the board, whether liberal or conservative. These facts are accepted unanimously because they're highly-evidenced and well-attested.[22] So, why begin with Christ instead of inspiration, inerrancy, or authority of Scripture? Habermas clues us in when he says, "a strong case can be made in favor of the principle that God verified Jesus's teachings by raising him from the dead. If Jesus taught that Scripture was God's message to us, then this would constitute a powerful reason for believers to do the same. And if Jesus utilized Scripture for his own ministry to others, believers should likewise do the same."[23] In other words, if God vindicated Jesus by raising Him from the dead, then God put His stamp of approval on Jesus' teachings. If Jesus believed and taught that Scripture is inspired and true, then we should believe that too! We have here a powerful reason for taking Scripture as inspired, true, and our final authority in all faith and practice.

Boyd and Habermas remain deeply committed to Scripture. Their point isn't that we should give up on or intentionally doubt doctrines such as inspiration and authority of Scripture; rather, amid their own doubts, they've come to realize that for their worldviews to stand they needed a strong theological center—Jesus Christ, the incarnate and raised Son of God. This sounds strikingly similar to Paul's own argument in 1 Corinthians 15 that if Jesus hasn't been raised from the dead, then our preaching is in vain, our faith is in vain and futile, and we're still lost in our sins (1 Cor 15:12-20). *Christ's resurrection is the litmus test for our faith*. Either Jesus is raised from the dead or He isn't. If He isn't, then Christianity is false. However, if Jesus has been raised from the dead, then Christianity is true!

---

[19]Ibid., 160-163.

[20]Gary R. Habermas, *The Risen Jesus and Future Hope* (Lanham, MD: Rowman and Littlefield, 2003), 213-224.

[21]Gary R. Habermas, "Evidential Apologetics," in *Five Views on Apologetics*, edited by Steven B. Cowan (Grand Rapids, MI: Zondervan, 2000), 99.

[22]Habermas, "Evidential Apologetics," 100.

[23]Habermas, *The Risen Jesus and Future Hope*, 213.

Coming to terms with doubt often requires a struggle and a lot of work, but it also requires having a solid theological center in the bedrock of one's noetic structure.

Sometimes, those wrestling with fact-based doubt have disordered thinking, including a faulty view of God. As Os Guinness reminds us, such doubts generally arise due to faulty presuppositions, whether they're pre-Christian or post-Christian. Faulty pre-Christian presuppositions are those presuppositions that remain a part of our noetic structures after coming to faith in Christ. Such presuppositions are dangerous, like Trojan Horses of the mind. Faulty post-Christian presuppositions are those presuppositions that enter into our thinking after faith. Like a frog being boiled slowly, these presuppositions often bring about our demise before we're even aware of it.[24] As Christians who struggle with doubt, we've got to root out these faulty presuppositions (see chapter four). That's why it's important that we know not only what it is that we believe, but why we believe what we do. Theology and apologetics are critical to this process.

Emotion-based Doubt

Having consider fact-based doubt, we shall now turn to emotion-based doubt. Unlike fact-based doubt, which is rooted in the mind and intellect, emotion-based doubt stems from emotional pain. Sometimes, those struggling with emotion-based doubt mask their doubt as an intellectual inquiry. But here's how you can tell the difference. Doubts that are more factually oriented go away once the person's questions have been answered. Emotion-based doubters, when presented with facts, often come back with phrases like: "I know that, but, what if . . ." or "yes, I understand that God loves me. He loves everyone. However, I still feel . . ." Habermas is insightful on this point: "Very regularly, the factual data is judged by how one *feels* about it, rather than on its own merits. Thus, instead of coming to grips with the strength of the evidence, the one experiencing the quandary often responds by emoting *about* it."[25] Giving emotion-based doubters more evidence is like throwing water on a grease fire. It doesn't bode well. For grease fires, you'll want to use a metal lid to cut off oxygen, or something like baking soda or a fire extinguisher to put it out. With emotional doubters, it requires a different tactic. The problem isn't the facts; *it's their emotions.*

How, then, do we help those struggling with emotion-based doubt? I recommend the following steps: (1) identify the lie, (2) replace it with the truth, and (3) change your thinking.[26] Let's begin with identifying the lie.

Step One: Identifying the Lie. Our emotions are powerful, gifts from God. Sometimes emotions help us to be bold; other times they keep us shriveled up in fear. But what's important to know about emotions, especially when helping those

---

[24]Guinness, *God in the Dark*, 63-64.

[25]Habermas, *Dealing with Doubt*, 64.

[26]I have adapted this strategy from Habermas, *Dealing with Doubt*, 73-83; William Backus and Marie Chapian, *Telling Yourself the Truth: Find Your Way Out of Depression, Anxiety, Fear, Anger, and Other Common Problems by Applying the Principles of Misbelief Therapy* (Bloomington, MN: Bethany House Publishing, 2000), 15.

struggling with emotional doubt, is their connection to our beliefs. How often do we get enraged at reports of child abuse, rape, or incest? Why do we get worked-up over acts of injustice and needless violence, or when people get bullied? *We get upset, worked-up, angered, and enraged because we believe such things are wrong!* The problem with emotion-based doubt, therefore, stems from forming wrong beliefs about things, which in turn affect our emotions. As William Backus and Marie Chapian point out in their book, *Telling Yourself the Truth*, "What you think and believe determines how you feel and what you do."[27] Emotions grounded in wrong beliefs wreak havoc on us, leading to painful doubt. To drive this point home, let me share my own story with doubt.

Several years ago, I struggled with anxiety, which brought doubt along with it. I was a third year Ph.D. student, a graduate assistant, and an adjunct instructor for more than one school—with a teaching load equivalent to full-time status—all the while, remaining active in my local church. Looking back, the signs for emotion-based doubt were clear. I wasn't getting enough sleep, I wasn't exercising, I was isolated from others due to working too much, and I felt a lot of pressure to perform well in meeting deadlines. At times, the pressure left me feeling debilitated. The more I tried to get things done, the less I accomplished. I knew I had a problem when my wife pointed out the constant counting on my fingers to see how much time I had left in the day to complete my work. On top of that I was an emoting mess!

One day, while talking my symptoms over with Dr. Gary Habermas, he recommended that I read *Telling Yourself the Truth*, by William Backus and Marie Chapian, the book mentioned earlier. That book revolutionized how I worked through my anxiety and doubt. What I didn't realize at the time, and what the book helped me to realize, is that I had a serious misbelief I was telling myself—a lie—which was at the root of my anxiety and doubt. I believed that the worst thing that could happen to me is not finishing my work. It's strange. The exact thought itself never crossed my mind; yet, it was deeply engrained in the way that I thought and perceived myself. This belief wreaked havoc on my emotions. I would often find myself saying things like, "I'm such a looser, why can't I get my work done." These thoughts even affected how I perceived God. Though I didn't doubt my salvation or whether or not God existed, it seemed as though God was distant and not listening to my prayers.

Step Two: Replace the Lie with the Truth. Once I found the root of the problem, the next thing I had to do was to replace the lie with the truth. The truth of the matter was, there were plenty of other things that were far worse than not meeting a deadline. Once I began to tell myself that, it's amazing how the anxiety began to disappear.

I've seen this same thing happen a different time in my life. As mentioned earlier, one area I struggled with as a teenager was over whether I was truly saved. Time and again I would ask God, "Lord, haven't I believed on you and repented of my sins? Why is there still sin in my life? How could you ever forgive me?" This

---

[27]Backus and Chapian, *Telling Yourself the Truth*, 22.

experience was deeply painful. I had a false belief about God. I believed that He couldn't forgive me. Through reading and prayer, I came to realize that salvation was a gift of God (Eph 2:8-9). It wasn't something to be earned. His grace was greater than my sin! When this finally began to sink in, it was freeing knowing that my salvation rested in God and not in myself. Knowing the truth brought me to a place where I could experience real freedom. Indeed, we truly are free in Christ, who is Himself the ground of all truth!

Step Three: Change Your Thinking. Often, emotion-based doubt comes from fear, worry, and anxiety. That was certainly true for me. But if anyone had reason to worry and to be anxious, it was the apostle Paul. Paul was shipwrecked, beaten, stoned, and imprisoned (2 Cor 11:23-27); yet, in his letter to the Philippians, he tells them not to be anxious. What was Paul's secret? To change the way we think! He lays out the following steps in Philippians 4:6-13:

Always rejoice in the Lord (4:6)

Take your requests to God (4:6)

Give thanks to God (4:6-7)

Replace negative thoughts with things that are "true," "honorable," "just," "pure," "lovely," and "commendable (4:8)

Put to practice what you've learned (4:9)

Be content in all circumstances (4:11-12)

Realize that strength comes from the Lord (4:13)

Paul realized that the Philippians couldn't change their circumstances, but they could change their beliefs about their circumstances. Worry generally stems from beliefs about our circumstances. Changing our beliefs about our circumstances goes a long way in helping us to overcome our doubts!

Theology and Doubt

To recap, we all struggle with doubt from time-to-time. Like a Trojan horse, doubt enters our thinking, crippling us, and keeping us from living the kind of life God has called us to—a life that's full and abundant. Though doubt can lead to sin or loss of faith, those outcomes aren't inevitable. We can be encouraged by the many saints who have gone on before us and who have come out on the other side of doubt. Sometimes, it requires that we stick it out and struggle through the pain, seeking earnestly the answers to our deepest longings, and trusting God in the midst of our uncertainty.

Theology and apologetics are crucial when wrestling with doubt. Sound theology provides a strong foundation for our beliefs, while apologetics supports the foundation. A well supported theology helps us in having an ordered worldview, uncorrupted by faulty presuppositions. Moreover, theology aids us in having a correct view of God. That's not to say that we can comprehend God. Surely, we cannot! However, we can apprehend what God has revealed to us about Himself and His plan for salvation.

Chapter Six

Becoming Living Sacrifices

GC² to the Core

Have you ever heard of GC²? Don't worry! It has nothing to do with math, but it does have everything to do with the heart of evangelical Christianity. GC² stands for the Great Commandments and the Great Commission.

> **Great Commandments**: "You shall love the Lord your God with all your heart and with all your soul and with all your mind. ^{38} This is the great and first commandment. ^{39} And a second is like it: You shall love your neighbor as yourself. ^{40} On these two commandments depend all the Law and the Prophets." (Mt 22:37-40)

> **Great Commission**: "All authority in heaven and on earth has been given to me. ^{19} Go therefore and make disciples of all nations, baptizing them in the name of the Father and of the Son and of the Holy Spirit, ^{20} teaching them to observe all that I have commanded you. And behold, I am with you always, to the end of the age." (Mt 28:18-20)

The previous three chapters placed emphasis on apologetics. Now we turn to the goal and mission of the church—loving God, loving others, and making disciples (hence GC²). Each of these are essentially related to theology. Theologians call this "practical theology." As we journey our way through the next four chapters, it's my desire you begin to see how important theology is to these areas of the Christian life. In this chapter, we begin zeroing in on the Greatest Commandment—loving God with all we have, which we'll continue more fully in chapter nine on worship. For now, we want to examine what it means to love God with our hearts and mind. We're also going to consider more fully the intimate connection between spiritual formation—especially the role of the renewal of the mind in becoming a living sacrifice—and theology. Our discussion here sets the foundation for the next three chapters.

Loving God in Heart and Mind

In the Greatest Commandment, Jesus tells us to love God "with all your heart and with all your soul and with all your mind." Essentially, Jesus is telling us that we are to love God with all we have. Not in part, but with our whole being—including our minds. Sadly, in efforts to emphasize the important role of faith, some Christians give more credence to loving God with their hearts (affections) over their minds. But Jesus' words here won't allow for it. Moreover, as discussed in chapter one, the task of theology is concerned with both scientia (knowledge) and sapientia (wisdom). Such a dichotomy between heart and mind is unwarranted. We are called to love God with our minds just as we're called to love God with our hearts.

So, what's the connection in all this? What's the relationship between the Greatest Commandment and spiritual formation? Moreover, how are we to understand the relationship between loving God with our hearts and mind and spiritual formation? Let's turn first to the Greatest command and spiritual formation, followed by a closer look at the biblical understanding of "heart" and "mind." As we make our way through each of these, hopefully the pieces will begin to come together.

The Greatest Commandment has much to teach us about discipleship (following Jesus) and spiritual formation (forming our character after Christ's). But most importantly it teaches us that our spiritual formation doesn't begin with us; rather, it begins with God! Full-front-and-center to our spiritual formation stands the eternal, holy, and good Creator God. Our story is ultimately a story about God. It's a story about a God who created us, made us in His image and likeness, loved us despite our rebellion, became incarnate and died for us, raised on behalf of us, forgave us despite our sin, and redeemed us by His unmerited grace and mercy. He is the God who, in the words of N.T. Wright, gets His "boots muddy" and His "hands bloody" in order "to put the world back to rights."[1] Sin distorts, God restores. Evil contorts, God reconciles. God is in the process of putting his good creation back into proper order. A proper understanding of spiritual formation, then, hinges on recognizing God's work in straightening us out and putting us back on the right path, in accordance with His original intentions and design plan. Because sin has distorted and corrupted every part of God's created order, including our hearts and minds, spiritual formation includes a recovery of our hearts and minds for God's intended purposes.

While we cannot do a full study of biblical anthropological terms, it's imperative to recognize that "heart" and "mind" in the Scriptures aren't as far apart from one another as people often think. Let's begin with the biblical notion of "heart." Though there are disagreements on human constitution (what makes up our human natures, whether we're just physical beings or whether we consist of both a body and soul), we can all agree that the Bible uses the notion of heart, metaphori-

---

[1]N. T. Wright, *Evil and the Justice of God* (Downers Grove, IL: InterVarsity Press, 2006), 59.

cally speaking, to refer to the innermost part of our person. Robert Pyne describes heart, in the biblical sense of the word, "[a]s the seat of emotion, understanding, will, and conscience, . . . the center of one's being, the source of all thoughts and behaviors."[2] Consider the following sampling of passages:

Keep your heart with all vigilance, for from it flow the springs of life. (Prv 4:23)

The mouth of the righteous is a fountain of life, but the mouth of the wicked conceals violence. (Prv 10:11)

If you say, "Behold, we did not know this," does not he who weighs the heart perceive it? Does not he who keeps watch over your soul know it, and will he not repay man according to his work? (Prv 24:12)

The fool says in his heart, "There is no God." They are corrupt, they do abominable deeds; there is none who does good. (Ps 14:1)

But as for those whose heart goes after their detestable things and their abominations, I will bring their deeds upon their own heads, declares the Lord God." (Ezk 11:21)

[34] You brood of vipers! How can you speak good, when you are evil? For out of the abundance of the heart the mouth speaks. [35] The good person out of his good treasure brings forth good, and the evil person out of his evil treasure brings forth evil. (Mt 12:34-35)

[15] And he said to them, "You are those who justify yourselves before men, but God knows your hearts. For what is exalted among men is an abomination in the sight of God. (Lk 16:15)

These passages make an organic connection between the state of our hearts and our actions. What comes out of us, both actions and words, show the state of our hearts. From the above passages, we also see that God knows our hearts, which can be intimidating or encouraging! Understanding that God knows our hearts holds us accountable to our actions, but it also gives us encouragement in knowing that even when others judge or accuse us wrongly, God knows the truth of hearts and actions.[3]

But what of thinking and the mind? Pyne gives a helpful overview:

Thinking usually takes place through the soul, spirit, or heart, but the New Testament also attributes it to the mind. The contents of the mind reflect the orientation of the heart, so the mind of the unbeliever is "set on the things of the flesh," is "hostile toward God," and "does not subject itself to the law of God" (Rom. 8:5, 7). Indeed, it is "not even able" to subject itself to God's law (8:7), for it is depraved (1 Tim. 6:5; 2 Tim 3:8), defiled (Titus 1:15), and blinded (2 Cor. 4:4). It needs to be

---

[2]Robert A. Pyne, *Humanity and Sin: The Creation, Fall, and Redemption of Humanity* (Nashville, TN: Word Publishing, 1999), 115.

[3]Ibid., 116.

opened to the truth (Luke 24:45) and renewed (Rom. 12:2; Eph. 4:23) so it will be set "on the things of the Spirit" (Rom. 8:5-6).[4]

If the thrust of Pyne's analysis is correct, then there's a significant relationship between our minds and our hearts. Our minds, which reflect "the orientation of the heart," need renewing—a topic to which we now turn.

What's in a Sacrifice?

In his letter to the Romans, Paul magisterially lays out an overview of God's plan for salvation. At the pivot point of the book—Paul's "so what" section—he appeals to his readers to become a "living sacrifice." Let's consider the passage in full:

> I appeal to you therefore, brothers, by the mercies of God, to present your bodies as a living sacrifice, holy and acceptable to God, which is your spiritual worship. [2] Do not be conformed to this world, but be transformed by the renewal of your mind, that by testing you may discern what is the will of God, what is good and acceptable and perfect. (Rom 12:1-2)

First off, it's important for us to note that presenting our bodies as living sacrifices is an act of worship. But what is it that we're to sacrifice? Our whole selves! That doesn't mean that we physically climb on an alter and deliver our bodies over as a sacrifice; rather, it's a spiritual act of worship that we offer up to God. Before, we were slaves to sin, but by God's grace we've been set free from the power and effects of sin on our lives. We've "become slaves of righteousness" (Rom 6:18), as Paul explains elsewhere:

> For just as you once presented your members as slaves to impurity and to lawlessness leading to more lawlessness, so now present your members as slaves to righteousness leading to sanctification. [20] For when you were slaves of sin, you were free in regard to righteousness. [21] But what fruit were you getting at that time from the things of which you are now ashamed? For the end of those things is death. [22] But now that you have been set free from sin and have become slaves of God, the fruit you get leads to sanctification and its end, eternal life. (Rom 6:19-22)

Second, Paul makes it clear that we are to be "transformed." But how are we to do this? Through the renewing of our minds! As N. T. Wright rightly (pun intended) reminds us, this self-offering to God should be directed through our minds.[5] He continues:

> Paul wants all Christians to have their minds renewed, so that they can think *in a different way*. . . . It won't do simply to go into autopilot and hope to get through somehow. . . . We have to be able to think about what to do—what to do with our whole lives, and what to do in the sudden crisis that faces us this very minute. Being trained to think "Christianly" is the necessary antidote to what will otherwise

[4]Ibid., 117.
[5]N. T. Wright, *After You Believe: Why Christian Character Matters* (New York: HaperOne, 2010), 149.

happen: being, as Paul says, "squeezed into the shape dictated by the present age."[6]

Thinking Christianly proves critical to avoiding conformity to the patterns of worldly thinking, and thus crucial to our spiritual formation.

Transforming the Mind

Having in the previous sections considered the relationship between mind and heart in the process of spiritual formation, and having shown the need for a renewed mind in offering ourselves to God as living sacrifices, now we see why the task of theology is important to discipleship and spiritual formation. The goal behind Christian theology isn't to become the smartest or the most intellectual among us. Moreover, as discussed in chapter one, theology isn't merely an intellectual enterprise. Christian theology is about transformation of the mind and heart, so that we can offer our whole selves to God as living sacrifices. We partake in the task of theology because we love God and want to follow hard after Him. We study theology because we aim to be disciples of Jesus Christ.

The first step in transforming the heart, then, is through the transformation of the mind. As Dallas Willard insightfully reminds us, the turn away from God first took place in our thinking, and it is through our thoughts "that the first movements toward the renovation of the heart occur."[7] Echoing Paul's remarks in Romans 12:1-2, he continues:

> NOW, CHRISTIAN SPIRITUAL FORMATION is inescapably a matter of recognizing in *ourselves* the idea system (or systems) of evil that governs the present age and the respective culture (or various cultures) that constitute life away from God. The needed transformation is very largely a matter of replacing in ourselves those idea systems of evil (and their corresponding cultures) with the idea system that Jesus Christ embodied and taught and with a culture of the Kingdom of God. This is truly a passage from darkness to light.[8]

Willard recognizes that, though such attempts to change our overall governing thoughts may prove difficult, it isn't impossible, especially with the help of divine intervention in our lives. Change comes through the person and Gospel of Jesus Christ. "The process of spiritual formation in Christ," he says, "is one of progressively replacing those destructive images and ideas with the images and ideas that filled the mind of Jesus himself,"[9] who is Himself the image of God. But how does this interchange of ideas come about? Through two avenues: "information" (i.e., facts) and "*our ability to think.*"[10]

Regarding information, we should orient our minds toward the truth. Jesus Himself proclaimed to be "the way, the truth, and the life" (Jn 14:6), and that by

---

[6]Ibid., 151.

[7]Dallas Willard, *Renovation of the Heart: Putting on the Character of Christ* (Colorado Springs, CO; NavPress, 2002), 95.

[8]Ibid., 98.

[9]Ibld., 101.

[10]Ibid., 102.

remaining in His word we know the truth, "and the truth will set you free" (Jn 8:32). Often, people have a poor understanding of God. And as we saw in the previous chapter, many of our doubts stem from an improper idea of what God is like. According to Willard, not knowing what God is like "destroys the soul, ruins society, and leaves people to eternal ruin."[11] Moreover, having a false view of God teeters on the edge of idolatry. Jesus' first task in His earthly ministry was to give people a proper perspective on God and to make known to them "the availability of eternal life from God through himself."[12]

As for thinking, Willard defines it in the following way: "the activity of searching out what *must* be true, or *cannot* be true, in light of the given facts and assumptions."[13] Proper thinking undermines distorted ideas and images we have. It brings clarity to our thinking, especially in regard to Jesus and the truth of the Gospel. Willard continues: "we must apply our thinking to and with the Word of God. We must thoughtfully take the Word in, dwell upon it, ponder its meaning, explore its implications—especially as it relates to our own lives. . . . We must *seek the Lord* by devoting our powers of thinking to understanding the facts and information of the gospel."[14]

Before moving on to our concluding section, it would be appropriate to consider one last question: how might we grow in our knowledge of God? Or, to put it differently, how might we engage in the process of renewing our minds? On this question, J. P. Moreland gives some helpful and practical advice: *"Be ruthless in assessing the precise nature and strength of what you actually believe and develop a specific plan of attack for improvement."*[15] In implementing this strategy, he gives three steps.

The first step includes locating and listing out our core beliefs (or, as we called them in the first chapter, *control beliefs*), and begin thinking hard over what we actually believe about them. In our assessment, we should be as clear and as concise as possible. He then asks his readers to consider the following questions: "Is it more of a slogan to you, or is it perhaps a vague, unclear string of words you utter in mantra-like fashion as a substitute for clear thinking about it? Or do you have a clear idea in your mind about the topic? Can you write on paper exactly what the topic means to you and what you think about it . . . ?"[16] Finally, for this first step, he suggests getting together with friends, spending the afternoon probing one another about each other's topics and what's actually believed about them.

The second step includes assessing how strongly we believe the things we do. Moreland even suggests assigning percentages to our beliefs. The goal is to be brutally honest with our answers. "Don't lie to yourself," says Moreland. Instead,

---

[11]Ibid., 103.

[12]Ibid.

[13]Ibid., 104.

[14]Ibid., 104-105.

[15]J. P. Moreland, *The Kingdom Triangle: Recover the Christian Mind, Renovate the Soul, Restore the Spirit's Power* (Grand Rapids, MI: Zondervan, 2007), 133.

[16]Ibid.

when "assessing the precise content and strength of your beliefs, you must distinguish what you say you believe from what you actually believe, what you want to believe from what you actually believe, how much you believe something from what you want others to think about the strength of your faith."[17]

Third, once we've taken these steps, it's important to implement a strategy to clarify and strengthen our beliefs. He suggests keeping a list of questions, doubts, or points of confusion on hand, actively seeking out people or books (and, I might add, the Scriptures) to help answer those areas that need clarifying. His final remarks on this are worth their weight in gold: "Read, think, ask questions, and keep checking things off your list. Don't settle for Christian slogans. Get real answers to your questions. Be a learner and see all this as an invitation to a journey of growth and confidence in knowledge."[18]

Moreland's steps are extremely helpful as we seek to grow in our knowledge of God. Whether we take his precise steps, or devise another method, it's imperative that we devote ourselves to rigorously studying and understanding our faith. But we must not leave it there. As Willard advised, we must also put into practice what we've learned. That's where the rubber meets the road, and a crucial part of following Jesus. But there is one other thing we can do—seek the Holy Spirit's help.

The Holy Spirit's role is crucial to the life of the believer and to the life of the Church, especially in helping us to understand the Scriptures. The technical term for this is *illumination*. Roy Zuck defines illumination in the following way: "the Spirit's work on the minds and hearts of believers that enables them not only to discern the truth but also to receive it, welcome it, and apply it."[19] The Holy Spirit is involved in aiding the believer, not only in the interpretive process, but also in understanding and applying the Scriptures. It's only appropriate that we seek help from the one who inspired the very words of Scripture we're trying to understand. Not only is the Holy Spirit the divine author of Scripture, but He's also the divine interpreter!

Theology and Spiritual Formation

Although Christians polarize when it comes to "head" knowledge and "heart" knowledge, the Bible stresses both. Not only should we have zeal and passion for God, but we should also love God with all our minds. Reflecting on Paul's charge to the Christians in Rome (Romans 12:1-2) and the Greatest Commandment, this chapter argued that the path to godly living and spiritual formation requires the task of transforming of the mind. Our beliefs impact our behavior, and theology plays a central role in the development of our minds.

---

[17]Ibid., 134.

[18]Ibid.

[19]Roy B. Zuck, "The Role of the Holy Spirit in Hermeneutics," in *Bibliotheca Sacra* 141 (1984), 129m accessed July 26, 2017, https://biblicalstudies.org.uk/article_spirit_zuck.html.

Chapter Seven

Building Character

Character, Who Needs It?

Perhaps you've heard it said, "character is what you do when no one else is looking." That's true, sort of. Character does have to do with being genuine and authentic in who we are, even when no one is around, but it can't be limited to that. After all, there are plenty of actions we do in private precisely because we don't want to draw attention to ourselves. Jesus says this much when he cautions us not to be like the hypocrites, who blow trumpets to let everyone know of their good deeds. Instead, when we give to the needy, we shouldn't let our left hand know what our right hand is doing; such actions should be done in secret (Mt 6:1-4). Moreover, we can think of people who act the same way, both in public and in private, but who, nevertheless, exhibit certain qualities that don't conform to the righteousness of Christ. These people are genuine, authentic, and *true to themselves*, but something's amiss. So, while character includes being genuine and authentic, both in private and in public, more is needed. All of us have a character. The question we must wrestle with is this: how should our characters be directed?

As Christians, our concern centers on having good character—a character that's modeled after Christ and molded by the Holy Spirit's work in our lives, and not merely a genuine and authentic character—though it certainly includes that! As we begin our thoughts on character, it might also prove helpful to consider what we don't mean by it.

What we don't mean by having good character is what Dallas Willard calls the "gospels of sin management," whereby it is taught that the heart of the Christian message centers only on dealing with sin.[1] Let me be clear (and as we'll discuss more in chapter eight): the Gospel is about the defeat of sin. Jesus, through His death and resurrection, conquered the effects and power of sin. However, what Willard warns against is making the whole of the Christian life about *our attempt at managing sin*. The task of sin management really is a grave misunderstanding that's infected our churches. The abundant and overcoming Christian life doesn't

---

[1] Dallas Willard, *The Divine Conspiracy: Rediscovering Our Hidden Life in God* (New York: HarperOne, 1997), 41.

come through our attempts at managing sin, but through a relationship with the Triune God (John 17:3). Christ has defeated sin and He's given us the Holy Spirit to overcome the power of sin in our lives. Consider Paul's words in his letter to the Ephesians:

> I do not cease to give thanks for you, remembering you in my prayers, [17] that the God of our Lord Jesus Christ, the Father of glory, may give you the Spirit of wisdom and of revelation in the knowledge of him, [18] having the eyes of your hearts enlightened, that you may know what is the hope to which he has called you, what are the riches of his glorious inheritance in the saints, [19] and what is the immeasurable greatness of his power toward us who believe, according to the working of his great might [20] that he worked in Christ when he raised him from the dead and seated him at his right hand in the heavenly places (Eph 1:16-20)

The key to living an abundant Christian life isn't found in managing our sin, but it's in recognizing and taking hold of what God has already accomplished in and for us through the life, death, and resurrection of Jesus Christ and through the empowering work of the Holy Spirit. According to Paul, that power working in us is the same "great might that he worked in Christ when he raised him from the dead!" Elsewhere, Paul writes:

> There is therefore now no condemnation for those who are in Christ Jesus. [2] For the law of the Spirit of life has set you free in Christ Jesus from the law of sin and death. [3] For God has done what the law, weakened by the flesh, could not do. By sending his own Son in the likeness of sinful flesh and for sin, he condemned sin in the flesh, [4] in order that the righteous requirement of the law might be fulfilled in us, who walk not according to the flesh but according to the Spirit. [5] For those who live according to the flesh set their minds on the things of the flesh, but those who live according to the Spirit set their minds on the things of the Spirit. [6] For to set the mind on the flesh is death, but to set the mind on the Spirit is life and peace. [7] For the mind that is set on the flesh is hostile to God, for it does not submit to God's law; indeed, it cannot. [8] Those who are in the flesh cannot please God.
>
> [9] You, however, are not in the flesh but in the Spirit, if in fact the Spirit of God dwells in you. Anyone who does not have the Spirit of Christ does not belong to him. [10] But if Christ is in you, although the body is dead because of sin, the Spirit is life because of righteousness. [11] If the Spirit of him who raised Jesus from the dead dwells in you, he who raised Christ Jesus from the dead will also give life to your mortal bodies through his Spirit who dwells in you. (Rom 8:1-11)

Note Paul's words here. *If we are in Christ, we are no longer condemned.* That means we no longer stand accused of our guilt before God because of Christ's finished work on the cross. Moreover, God's Spirit, who is at work in us, has set us free "from the law of sin and death." God accomplished through the finished work of Christ and by the sending of the Spirit what the Law (the Mosaic Law), though good and holy (Rom 7:12), could not.

Furthermore, we must realize that righteousness never comes through following the Law. As already noted, the Law is good and holy. It was God's gift until the giving of the Messiah, but it could never impart life. Rather, it served as our tutor, leading us to Christ. By becoming a curse for us, Christ freed us from the curse of the law, bringing about God's promises, so that we might receive the promised Holy Spirit. We are justified (declared righteous) before God, and we receive the Spirt, not by following the Law, but by faith (Gal 3:10-29).[2]

When we think of good character, then, it's intricately connected to what God is doing in us. It is the product of God's Spirit. We now look further into the Holy Spirit's work in us to produce good character by examining the fruit of the Spirit.

The Fruit of the Spirit

In his letter to the Galatians, the apostle Paul uses a farming metaphor—the "fruit of the Spirit—to speak about the Holy Spirit's cultivating work in the life of believers. Let's consider the passage and then explore the fruit a bit more in depth.[3]

> [16]But I say, walk by the Spirit, and you will not gratify the desires of the flesh. [17]For the desires of the flesh are against the Spirit, and the desires of the Spirit are against the flesh, for these are opposed to each other, to keep you from doing the things you want to do. [18]But if you are led by the Spirit, you are not under the law. [19]Now the works of the flesh are evident: sexual immorality, impurity, sensuality, [20]idolatry, sorcery, enmity, strife, jealousy, fits of anger, rivalries, dissensions, divisions, [21]envy, drunkenness, orgies, and things like these. I warn you, as I warned you before, that those who do such things will not inherit the kingdom of God. [22]But the fruit of the Spirit is love, joy, peace, patience, kindness, goodness, faithfulness, [23]gentleness, self-control; against such things there is no law. [24]And those who belong to Christ Jesus have crucified the flesh with its passions and desires. [25]If we live by the Spirit, let us also keep in step with the Spirit. (Gal 5:16-25)

Paul begins by clarifying that there's a real internal struggle going on in each of us between two competing desires—the desires of Spirit and the desires of the flesh. Mixing the two is like mixing water and oil. If you've ever tried mixing the two, you know that the oil always floats to the top. The two simply do not mix. The same goes with our spiritual lives. The desires of the Spirit and the desires of the flesh are opposed to one another and the two don't mix. Paul's charge to the believers of Galatia is to "walk by the Spirit." By doing so, we won't give in to the desires of the flesh.

If we belong to Christ, then we've "crucified the flesh with its passions and desires," that is to say, we've said "no" to our earthly desires, and we've turned from them to Christ. As Paul says elsewhere in the same letter, "I have been crucified with Christ. It is no longer I who live, but Christ who lives in me. And the life I now live in the flesh I live by faith in the Son of God, who loved me and gave himself for me" (Gal 2:20). As those who live by faith and who are keeping "in step with the Spirit," we are to have within us certain characteristics or, to put it

---

[2]N. T. Wright, *After You Believe: Why Christian Character Matters* (New York: HaperOne, 2010), 192.

[3]The material in this section on the fruit of the Spirit began through a series of web articles I wrote for Fervr.net, which can be found by taking the following web link: http://fervr.net/author/37312/.

differently, virtues—love, joy, peace, patience, kindness, goodness, faithfulness, gentleness, and self-control—produced in us by the Spirit. Let's consider each in turn.

Love. The first virtue on the list is love, and for good reason. Of the virtues listed out, love is the only one that has a full chapter dedicated to it (1 Cor 13). Furthermore, as we saw in chapter six, the great commandments include loving God with all that we have and loving our neighbors as ourselves (Mt 22:37; Mk 12:30; Lk 10:27; cf. Dt 6:4). On multiple occasions throughout the New Testament, we're told that loving God and one's neighbor sums up the whole law (Mt 22:40; Rom 13:10; Gal 5:14).

The biblical understanding of love is often misunderstood by modern Western culture. It's not merely a feeling or emotion, nor is it essentially sexual in nature. We don't fall into it, as often portrayed in love ballads or on movies. C. S. Lewis is surely correct when he says, "love, in the Christian sense, does not mean an emotion. It is a state not of the feelings but of the will; that state of the will which we have naturally about ourselves, and must learn to have about other people."[4] In discussing the command to love one's neighbor, philosopher Francis Howard-Snyder provides some helpful insight:

> The second great commandment is like the first. It is fair to assume that the love we owe our neighbor is of the same kind as the love we owe God. Our love for God ought to include an appreciation of him and a desire for union with him, in addition to a desire that his will be done. If our love for our neighbor is to be like the love we owe God, this suggests that the love we have for our neighbors should involve the same elements. Indeed, it makes sense that our love for other people should not be simply benevolence or sheer concern for their well-being, but should also involve desires to be related to them, and an appreciation of what is valuable in them, and enjoyment of them. For if one's attitude toward others was solely that of benevolence, it would seem that one wouldn't want anything they have to offer. Sheer benevolence looks like a kind of arrogance, an attitude of independence and inequality vis-à-vis our neighbors.[5]

Howard-Snyder's words echo the words of Paul when he says, "If I give away all I have, and if I deliver up my body to be burned, but have not love, I gain nothing" (1 Cor 13:3). Love, then, doesn't have to do merely with charity and self-sacrifice, though it certainly may include those. How, then, should we think of the biblical view of love? Paul sketches it out in the following way:

> Love is patient and kind; love does not envy or boast; it is not arrogant [5] or rude. It does not insist on its own way; it is not irritable or resentful; [6] it does not rejoice at wrongdoing, but rejoices with the truth. [7] Love bears all things, believes all things, hopes all things, endures all things. (1 Cor 13:4-7)

There are four attributes we can take away from this:

---

[4] C. S. Lewis, *Mere Christianity* (New York: HarperSanFrancisco, 1980), 129.

[5] Francis Howard-Snyder, "Christian Ethics," in *Reason for the Hope Within*, edited by Michael J. Murray (Grand Rapids, MI: William B. Eerdmans, 1999), 387-388.

Love is a choice

Love is an attitude

Love is active

Love is selfless[6]

Lastly, we love because God first loved us (1 Jn 4:19). The Elder of 1 John tells us that "God is love" (1 Jn 4:8, 16) and that he demonstrated His love towards us in sending Christ to die for our sins (1 Jn 4:10). Paul says something similar in his letter to the Romans:

> For while we were still weak, at the right time Christ died for the ungodly. [7] For one will scarcely die for a righteous person—though perhaps for a good person one would dare even to die— [8] but God shows his love for us in that while we were still sinners, Christ died for us. (Rom 5:6-8)

Christ set the example for us. He who knew no sin, humbled himself, taking on our humanity and bearing the shame of the cross, suffered on our behalf (2 Cor 5:21; Phil 2:5-8; Hb 4:15; 1 Jn 3:5; 1 Pt 1:18-19).

Joy. Often, people mistake joy for happiness. However, there's quite a difference. Happiness in today's culture has mostly to do with pleasure and not in the sense Aristotle meant it, that is, as something akin to human flourishing.[7] Happiness is temporary and fleeting, and it is often based on our circumstances. Joy, on the other hand, is not. Joy stems from the well springs of our hearts, pouring out into our daily lives, despite our circumstances. In the Psalms, joy is often connected with singing (Ps 47:1; 63:7; 81:1; 84:2; 95:1, 2; 100:1; 105:43) and with salvation (Ps 71:23). Joy results from a life filled with the Holy Spirit (Acts 13:52; Rom 14:17; 1 Thes 1:6), and, as we'll see below, full of contentment and thanksgiving.

Throughout the Scriptures, God's people are commanded to be joyful (Ps 32:11; 33:1; 35:27; 66:1; Phil 4:4), even during our trials. Take the words from James, the brother of our Lord:

> Count it all joy, my brothers, when you meet trials of various kinds, [3] for you know that the testing of your faith produces steadfastness. [4] And let steadfastness have its full effect, that you may be perfect and complete, lacking in nothing. (Js 1:2-4)

Being joyful in the middle of our trials is hard to do, but the purpose in it is so that we might become "perfect and complete, lacking nothing." What James means here is that through persevering during our trials, we become mature (perfect) in our faith. Consider what Paul says on this:

---

[6]Ronnie Campbell, "What is Love?" April 7, 2015 http://fervr.net/bible/what-is-love1, accessed July 31, 2017.

[7]Aristotle, "Nicomachean Ethics," in *Greek Philosophy: Thales to Aristotle*, ed. Reginald E. Allen (New York: The Free Press, 1966), 262-374.

I rejoiced in the Lord greatly that now at length you have revived your concern for me. You were indeed concerned for me, but you had no opportunity. [11] Not that I am speaking of being in need, for I have learned in whatever situation I am to be content. [12] I know how to be brought low, and I know how to abound. In any and every circumstance, I have learned the secret of facing plenty and hunger, abundance and need. [13] I can do all things through him who strengthens me. (Phil 4:10-13)

Though he had suffered tremendously for the Lord, he learned that the secret to having joy in his life, despite his circumstances, is found in two things: *contentment* and *Christ's strength*.

Peace. We live in a world full of turmoil. All one needs to do is turn on the local or national news. Politicians fighting over policy, nations at war, and countries filled with civil unrest. Our world is filled with strife. Is there any hope? For Christians, the answer is yes! And not only that, we can find peace now.

Peace is ultimately found in the good news of the Gospel (Rom 5:1). At one time, we were alienated from and hostile to God in our minds, but Christ reconciled us to God through "his body of flesh by his death" (Col 1:21). It is "by the blood of his cross" that He is "making peace," and will ultimately reconcile all things to Himself, things both in heaven and on earth.

In his letter to the Philippians, Paul tells us that we shouldn't be anxious about anything; rather, we should present our requests to God with thankfulness (Phil 4:6). In so doing, "the peace of God, which surpasses all understanding, will keep your hearts and your minds in Christ Jesus" (Phil 4:7).

Patience. Our world is changing at a rapid pace. We're constantly being bombarded with the newest and the latest gadget. The latest cellphone. The latest computer. The latest gaming system. It's a struggle just to keep up with it all. Moreover, in the West, we have become accustomed to instant gratification. Often, we're like the spoiled child who screams "I want it, and I want it now!" Everything is at our fingertips. When I was younger, I often had to listen to the radio for hours or days just to hear a new song on the radio. Now we can pull up Spotify or YouTube and have it available instantly. For many of us, we've lost the ability to be patient.

The Bible has much to say about patience. First, we see that patience is connected to perseverance. If you recall from our earlier discussion on joy, James calls us to persevere during our trials. In so doing, we build perseverance, and through perseverance we move on to Christian maturity (Js 1:2-4). Paul, in his letter to the Romans, says something similar:

Not only that, but we rejoice in our sufferings, knowing that suffering produces endurance, [4] and endurance produces character, and character produces hope, [5] and hope does not put us to shame, because God's love has been poured into our hearts through the Holy Spirit who has been given to us. (Rom 5:3-5)

Second, we can learn from others who have persevered. Consider Abraham who, at the age of 75, God promised a child to be his heir. That promise wasn't fulfilled until he was at the ripe old age of 100 (Gen 21:5). Yet, despite this, he did not waiver. Rather, during this time he "grew strong in his faith as he gave glory to God, fully convinced that God was able to do what he had promised" (Rom 4:20-21). Talk about perseverance! The writer of Hebrews lists out many of the saints from Scripture who by faith waited patiently for God's promise of hope, persevering at times to the point of persecution and death, and yet, who did not experience the promise in their lifetimes (Heb 11:4-39). They were commended for their faith!

Kindness. Have you ever been around an unpleasant person, someone who complains incessantly, has a short fuse, or nags a lot? It can be like fingernails digging into a chalkboard. Unbearable! Quite the opposite is true for a genuinely kind person. Nine-times-out-of-ten we would prefer to be around the kind person.

As Christians, we're called to a life of kindness (Gal 5:22; Eph 4:32; Col 3:12), not just to our friends and family, but also to our enemies. According to Jesus, we're to love our enemies, do good to them, and lend our possessions, while expecting nothing in return. Why should we do this? Because God is Himself kind, even to those who are "ungrateful" and "evil" (Lk 6:35). In reflecting kindness in our lives, we emulate the very character of God. After all, God's offer of salvation through the Gospel is itself a display of His kindness to us. Considering the following passages:

> But when the goodness and loving kindness of God our Savior appeared, ⁵ he saved us, not because of works done by us in righteousness, but according to his own mercy, by the washing of regeneration and renewal of the Holy Spirit, ⁶ whom he poured out on us richly through Jesus Christ our Savior (Ti 3:4-6).

> So that in the coming ages he might show the immeasurable riches of his grace in kindness toward us in Christ Jesus. ⁸ For by grace you have been saved through faith. And this is not your own doing; it is the gift of God, ⁹ not a result of works, so that no one may boast. (Eph 2:7-9)

It's because of God's kindness that Jesus came into the world, cleansed us through the Holy Spirit, and offers us eternal hope. Furthermore, God's kindness leads us to repentance (Rom 2:4).

Finally, our attitude should be like Christ's (Phil 2:5). When examining the Gospels, time and again we see kindness displayed throughout the life of Jesus. One of the most beautiful narratives in the Scripture is centered on a miraculous act of Jesus, but it also shows His kindness toward those to whom He ministered. The Gospel writer, Luke, tells us that after arriving at a town called Nain, Jesus observed a mother grieving over the loss of her only son. Upon seeing her, He had compassion on her and brought her son back to life. The word "compassion" carries the idea of being moved by one's inner parts. The NIV captures the idea best when it says, "his heart when out to her." (Luke 7:11-16). All that Jesus did, including His miracles, He did to bring glory to the Father. In this instance, in bringing the young man back to life, not only did He bring glory to the Father, but He also demonstrated the kindness of God.

Goodness. How often do you hear people say things like?

"haters gonna hate"

"it's a dog-eat-dog world"

"survival of the fittest"

"don't be a goody two-shoes"

"win at all costs"

"might as well live it up, you only live once"

"it's my life, I'll live how I want to"

Such sayings often reflect the inner-most part of who we are—the heart. Unfortunately, what many Christians don't realize when they use these popular sayings is that they're buying into non-Christian ideologies. As Christians, we're called to a life of goodness. We're to do good in the world, not evil. Paul captures this idea well in his letter to the Romans. In the last chapter, we discussed offering our bodies as living sacrifices, which begins with the renewing of our minds (Rom 12:1-2). In what follows, Paul outlines what that looks like. In the middle of his discussion, we find Paul saying things like:

"Abhor what is evil: hold fast to what is good" (v. 9)

"Outdo one another in showing honor" (v. 10)

"Contribute to the needs of the saints and seek to show hospitality" (v. 13)

"Bless those who persecute you; bless them and do not curse them" (v. 14)

"Live in harmony with one another" (v. 16)

"Associate with the lowly" (v. 16)

"Repay no evil for evil, but give thought to do what is honorable in the sight of all" (v. 17)

"as far as it depends on you, live peaceably with all" (v. 18)

"never avenge yourselves, but leave it to the wrath of God" (v. 19)

"If your enemy is hungry, feed him; if he is thirsty, give him something to drink" (v. 20)

"Do not overcome by evil, but overcome evil with good" (v. 21)

Wow, what a contrast! What would it look like if we Christians were to replace the worldly slogans and put into action the ones Paul gives us in this passage.

Think of the difference that would make in our own spheres of influence—families, friendships, churches, schools, and communities.

The central reason we should be good stems from the fact that God is Himself Good. The short letter of 1 John tells us that "God is light, and in him is no darkness at all" (1 Jn 1:5). The Elder John is using the word "light" as a metaphor. By it, He means that God is perfect moral goodness. John's point isn't merely the fact that God's actions are always good. Though that's certainly true, he's going for something much stronger. God always does good because God *is in His every nature Good*. God's goodness becomes the ground for our own goodness. When we walk in the light, says John, we "practice the truth" and "have fellowship with one another," that is to say, we have fellowship with God and with other Christians (1 Jn 1:6-7).

Let's be clear, none of us are good on our own (Rom 3:10). We all fall short of God's standard (Rom 3:23). God alone is Good (Mk 10:18-19). Yet, because of Christ's work we've been set free from the power of sin and death in our lives (Rom 6:18; 8:2), purified from our unrighteousness (1 Jn 1:7), become "new creations" in Christ (2 Cor 5:17), and given the power to overcome sin in order to live holy lives (Rom 8:9-15; Eph 1:18-20). Though God saves us by His grace through faith, apart from any good works (Eph 2:8-9), we are, nevertheless, God's "workmanship, created in Christ Jesus for good works" (Eph 2:10).

Faithfulness. Are you more of a cat person or a dog person? My family and I prefer cats; yet, one thing I admire about dogs is their faithfulness. I'm reminded of the song, "Lord, please help me to be the kind of person my dog thinks I am."[8] Dogs are extremely loyal to their owners. How much more should we Christians be loyal to our Lord?

Again, as with many of the other fruit, they're grounded in the very character of God, and the reason that we should be faithful is because God Himself is faithful (1 Cor 1:9). Theologians have long thought of God as immutable—the idea that God doesn't change. There are disagreements about what immutability means, but minimally it refers to God not changing in His character (Heb 13:8; Mal 3:6). Paul tells his young apprentice, Timothy, that even when we're unfaithful God remains faithful because He can't deny Himself (2 Tim 2:13). Thankfully, God's faithfulness to us doesn't hinge on our faithfulness to Him! Furthermore, throughout Scripture we're told that God's faithfulness is immense (Ps 36:5; 89:8), doesn't run out (Ps 119:90), never fails (Lam 3:22-23), and is like a shield and place of refuge (Ps 91:4). Even when we mess things up, God is faithful to forgive us of our sins (1 Jn 1:9). Lastly, God aids us in escaping temptation, giving us the ability to endure through it (1 Cor 10:13).

Gentleness. In the Summer of 2016 we added a new member to our growing family. Our then four-year old often needed reminded that he couldn't play with his younger brother the same way he did with his older siblings. Instead, he had

---

[8]The Bellamy Brothers, "Lord Help Me Be the Kind of Person (My Dog Thinks I Am)" from the album *Jesus is Coming*, Curb records, 2007.

to be gentle with him. In the same way, we Christians need reminding that gentleness makes up part of our spiritual DNA.

We don't often think of gentleness as a virtue, but it is among those listed by Paul as a fruit of the Spirit. In the New Testament, various passages dealing with gentleness place it within the context of interacting with other people. For example, when correcting those who are caught in sin, Paul tells us that those "who are spiritual should restore him in a spirit of gentleness" (Gal 5:23). The same is true when correcting those who oppose us (2 Tim 2:25). As discussed in our chapter on defending the faith, Peter tells us that we should "make a defense to anyone who asks" us with "gentleness and respect" (1 Pet 3:15). Finally, Paul exhorts believers "to speak evil of no one, to avoid quarreling, to be gentle, and to show perfect courtesy toward all people (Ti 3:2).

Self-control. So far, we've made our way through each of the other eight fruits, but there's one more we must consider—self-control. As we've seen throughout, the role of the Holy Spirit in our spiritual development is crucial. We cannot build character and become mature Christians apart from the work of the Holy Spirit in our lives. Nevertheless, it does take some work on our part, as this last fruit—self-control—suggests. N. T. Wright explains it well:

> The key is this: the "fruit of the Spirit" *does not grow automatically.* The nine varieties of fruit do not suddenly appear just because someone has believed in Jesus, has prayed for God's Spirit, and has then sat back and waited for "fruit" to arrive. Oh, there may well be strong and sudden initial signs that fruit is on the way. Many new Christians, particularly when a sudden conversion has meant a dramatic turning away from a lifestyle full of the "works of the flesh," report their own astonishment at the desire that springs up within them to love, to forgive, to be gentle, to be pure. Where, they ask, has all this come from? . . . These are the blossoms; to get to the fruit you have to be a gardener. You have to discover how to tend and prune, how to irrigate the field, how to keep birds and squirrels away. You have to watch for blight and mold, cut away ivy and other parasites that suck the life out of the tree, and make sure the young trunk can stand firm in strong winds. Only then will the fruit appear.[9]

How often have we seen in our discussion so far words like "persevere" or "endure" connected to the various fruit? By no means does that me we can earn our salvation or that we're even doing it through our own strength. What we do we do because of the grace of God and in and through the empowering work of the Holy Spirit (Rom 8:9-15; Eph 1:18-20). We truly are, as Paul says in Ephesians 2:10, created in Christ Jesus for good works!

Takeaway. As we've made our way through each of the fruit of the Spirit, hopefully you've begun to see familiar themes. One such theme is that God never promises us an easy life. We're called to press on and to persevere, even during our trials. God doesn't expect anything less from us than what He expected from His Son. The writer of Hebrews understood this when he tells us that the Lord disciplines those he loves. He goes on to say:

---

[9]Wright, *After You Believe*, 195-196.

It is for discipline that you have to endure. God is treating you as sons. For what son is there whom his father does not discipline? [8] If you are left without discipline, in which all have participated, then you are illegitimate children and not sons. [9] Besides this, we have had earthly fathers who disciplined us and we respected them. Shall we not much more be subject to the Father of spirits and live? [10] For they disciplined us for a short time as it seemed best to them, but he disciplines us for our good, that we may share his holiness. [11] For the moment all discipline seems painful rather than pleasant, but later it yields the peaceful fruit of righteousness to those who have been trained by it. (Heb 12:7-11)

We can take courage from Christ who "learned obedience through what he suffered" (Heb 5:8). Moreover, it is through Christ that we receive our strength to endure during our time with suffering (Phil 4:13). We are promised that He will never leave us nor forsake us (Heb 13:5). It is through our suffering, patience, and perseverance that we become mature Christians.

We also find that God is the ground for the fruit in our lives. Reflecting on God's character, we see that God *is love* and loving toward us (1 Jn 4:8), finds joy in His creation (Gen 1:4, 10, 12, 17, 21, 25, 31; Neh 8:10; 1 Tim 1:9-11), brings peace to His followers (Jud 6:24; Rom 15:33; 16:20; 1 Cor 14:33; 2 Cor 13:11; Phil 4:9; 2 The 3:16; Heb 13:20), demonstrates patience in His dealings with His creatures (Ex 34:6; Nub 14:18; Ps 86:15; Rom 2:4; 2 Pt 3:9, 15), offers kindness to us (Ps 17:7; 63:3; 117:2; Is 63:7; Rom 2:4; Eph 27: Tt 3:4-6), grounds all that is good and displays His goodness to all people in various ways (Lev 11:44; Js 1:17; 1 Pt 1:16; 1 Jn 1:5), remains faithful to His people (Dt 7:9; Ps 33:4; 86:15; 1 Cor 10:13; 2 Thes 3:3; 2 Tim 2:13; Heb 10:23; 11:11), acts gently toward us (Ps 18:35; Mt 11:28-30), and stays constant (self-controlled) in His character and dealings with humans (1 Sam 15:29; Ps 102:12, 25-28; Mal 3:6; Js 1:17; Heb 13:7-9). As Christians, we're ultimately called to be imitators of God and of Christ (1 Cor 11:1; Eph 5:1-2; Phil 2:5). Practicing the fruit in our lives reflects God to the world.

Spirituality and the Disciplines

So far, we've been talking a lot about what good character looks like from the Christian-life-and-worldview. Before closing out this chapter, it would be beneficial to reflect on the nature of spirituality and what it means to partake in the spiritual disciplines.

As noted in chapter four, culture constantly bombards us with competing ideas, and there's much ambiguity about spirituality in our current cultural climate. Regarding this, J. P. Moreland insightfully writes:

> Spirituality is in, but no one knows which form to embrace. Indeed, the very idea that one form may be better than another seems arrogant and intolerant. A flat stomach is of greater value than a mature character. The makeup man is more important than the speech writer. People listen, or pretend to listen, to what actors—*actors!*—have to say! [10]

---

[10] J. P. Moreland, *Kingdom Triangle: Recover the Christian Mind, Renovate the Soul,*

Sadly, Christians, too, are often confused about spirituality and the practice of spiritual disciplines. What does it mean to be "spiritual"? What does that look like in the life of the Christian?

First, to be "spiritual" in the biblical sense means that a person must be a Christian, not in name only, but by having entered a saving relationship with the one, true, and living God—the God who washes and cleanses us from our sins (1 Cor 6:11; Ti 3:6; 1 Jn 7; Heb 10:22), who redeems and reconciles us to Himself (Col 1:20), and who gives us the precious Holy Spirit (Jn 14:15-31) to empower us to live out the Christian life. In other words, we must be "born again" (Jn 3:3). It's what the Scriptures call "eternal" or "abundant" life. In the Gospel of John, when praying to the Father, Jesus says, "this is eternal life, that they know you, the only true God, and Jesus Christ whom you have sent" (Jn 17:3). The idea of "know" refers to an intimate, personal knowledge, and not merely a belief. In other words, we must have a personal, intimate relationship with God. True spirituality, then, pours out from being born again and in having a right relationship with the Triune God—Father, Son, and Holy Spirit.[11]

Second, to be spiritual, as prescribed by Scripture (and as considered earlier), we must live by and keep in step with the Spirit, cultivating His fruit in our lives (Gal 5:16-25). Some people equate spirituality with a list of do's and don'ts, but as Francis Schaeffer pointed out many years ago, spirituality is connected to who we are and the striving to be a certain kind of person, not so much performing a certain "list" of things. True spirituality, says Schaeffer, "is more than refraining from a certain list of external taboos in a mechanical way."[12] Rather than an outward way of doing things, true spirituality is inward, which we begin to see through the last of the ten commandments, "do not covet."[13] The command not to covet is the "hub" of the whole set of commandments. It is this commandment that we break before any of the others. So, in breaking any one of the commandments, we are also breaking the command not to covet. The command not to covet is "negative." It is the opposite side of the positive commands to love God with all that we have and to love our neighbors (Dt 6:4; Lv 19:18; Mk 12:29-31; Mt 22:37, 39), both of which are "internal," and not external in nature. On this point, Schaeffer explains:

> We must see that to love God with all the heart, mind, and soul is not to covet against God; and to love man, to love our neighbors as ourselves, is not to covet against man. When I do not love the Lord as I should, I am coveting against the Lord. And when I do not love my neighbor as I should, I am coveting against him.[14]

Restore the Spirit's Power (Grand Rapids, MI: Zondervan, 2007), 12.

[11]Francis A. Schaeffer, *True Spirituality* (Wheaton, IL: Tyndale House Publishers, 1971), 3.

[12]Ibid., 5.

[13]Ibid., 6.

[14]Ibid., 7.

True spirituality, then, is an inward disposition toward God, which includes being content in Him, no matter our circumstances. Having briefly considered the nature of spirituality, we now turn to spiritual discipline.

In his book, *The Kingdom Triangle*, J. P. Moreland outlines, what he takes to be a significant problem people in our culture face, including many Christians. He calls it "the empty self, which has the following traits:

The empty self is inordinately individualistic

The empty self is infantile

The empty self is narcissistic

The empty self is passive[15]

Moreland provides two anecdotes for moving away from the empty self: self-denial (Mt 16:24-26) and spiritual disciplines (Rom 6:6-11, 19; 12:1-2; Col 3:5; 1 Tim 4:7-8).[16] Regarding self-denial, consider what Jesus said to those who follow Him:

If anyone would come after me, let him deny himself and take up his cross and follow me. [25] For whoever would save his life will lose it, but whoever loses his life for my sake will find it. [26] For what will it profit a man if he gains the whole world and forfeits his soul? Or what shall a man give in return for his soul? (Mt 16:24-26)

Jesus' words are hard hitting. It's not about us! We're to be willing to give it all up for Christ.

Regarding Scripture's mandate on spiritual disciplines, Moreland asks us to mull over the following passages:

I appeal to you therefore, brothers, by the mercies of God, to present your bodies as a living sacrifice, holy and acceptable to God, which is your spiritual worship. (Rom 12:1)

Put to death therefore what is earthly in you: sexual immorality, impurity, passion, evil desire, and covetousness, which is idolatry. (Col 3:5)

Have nothing to do with irreverent, silly myths. Rather train yourself for godliness; [8] for while bodily training is of some value, godliness is of value in every way, as it holds promise for the present life and also for the life to come. (1 Tim 4:7-8)

He suggests the above passages provide four concepts in relation to spiritual disciplines:

Habits – "an ingrained tendency to act, think, or feel a certain way without need to choose to do so."[17]

[15]Moreland, *Kingdom Triangle*, 142-143.
[16]Ibid., 147 &149.
[17]Ibid., 150.

Character – "the sum total of one's habits, good and bad."[18]

Flesh – "the sinful tendencies of habits that reside in the body and whose nature is opposite of the Kingdom of God."[19]

Body – "one's living, animated physical aspect."[20]

Thus, when we consider passages such as Romans 12:1, we are to understand that it calls for more than a one-time action on the part of the believer, but, rather, it involves "habitual, repeated bodily exercises (1 Cor. 9:23-27; 1 Tim. 4:7-8) involving specific body parts (Rom. 6:11-13, 19) and resulting in putting to death one's bad habits."[21]

So, what are "spiritual disciplines." We might define a spiritual discipline as *any habit within the Christian life that propels a person toward living a content and thankful life before God, a life separated from sin through the giving up of the self, and one that joys in the pleasures of the eternal and almighty God.* Moreland suggests two kinds of kinds disciplines:

Disciplines of abstinence: solitude, silencing, fasting, frugality, chastity, secrecy, sacrifice

Disciplines of engagement: study, worship, celebration, service, prayer, fellowship, confession, and submission[22]

For lack of space, we cannot here consider each of these disciplines. For now, I'll briefly highlight the biblical emphasis on the use of spiritual disciplines. Jesus Himself practiced the disciplines. We regularly see Jesus fasting (Lk 4:1), praying in solitude (Mk 1:35-39; Lk 4:42), and living out a life of submission to the Father (Phil 2:8; Heb 5:8). Moreover, Scripture emphasizes and commands the following disciplines:

Worship and celebration (1 Cor 14:26; Eph 5:19; Col 3:16)

Fellowship (Heb 10:24)

Confession (Js 5:16; 1 Jn 1:9)

Simplicity (Mt 6:19-21, 25-34; 1 Tim 6:6-10

Study (2 Tim 2:16)

Meditation (Phil 4:8)

---

[18]Ibid.
[19]Ibid., 151.
[20]Ibid., 150.
[21]Ibid., 152.
[22]Ibid., 153.

Sacrifice (Rom 12:1-2; 14:1-15; 1 Cor 10:23-33)

Charity (1 Tim 5:3-5; Js 1:27; 2:14-17; 1 Jn 16-18)

In the book of Acts, we see that the early church practiced the disciplines. Consider the following two passages:

> And they devoted themselves to the apostles' teaching and the fellowship, to the breaking of bread and the prayers. [43] And awe came upon every soul, and many wonders and signs were being done through the apostles. [44] And all who believed were together and had all things in common. [45] And they were selling their possessions and belongings and distributing the proceeds to all, as any had need. [46] And day by day, attending the temple together and breaking bread in their homes, they received their food with glad and generous hearts, [47] praising God and having favor with all the people. And the Lord added to their number day by day those who were being saved. (Acts 2:42-47)

> Now the full number of those who believed were of one heart and soul, and no one said that any of the things that belonged to him was his own, but they had everything in common. [33] And with great power the apostles were giving their testimony to the resurrection of the Lord Jesus, and great grace was upon them all. [34] There was not a needy person among them, for as many as were owners of lands or houses sold them and brought the proceeds of what was sold [35] and laid it at the apostles' feet, and it was distributed to each as any had need. (Acts 4:32-35)

From these passages, we see several disciplines were emphasized among the earliest Christian community:

> Study, fellowship, and prayer: "devoted themselves to the apostles' teaching and the fellowship, to the breaking of bread and the prayers" and "all who believed were together and had all things in common"

> Celebration and worship: "filled with awe," "praising God," "attending the temple together," and "received their food with glad and generous hearts"

> Simplicity and service: "selling their possessions and belongings," "had all things in common," and "for as many as were owners of lands or houses sold them and brought the proceeds of what was sold"

> Charity: "distributing the proceeds to all, as any had need," "not a needy person among them"

Moreover, we see that the disciplines were not merely individualistic endeavors, but corporate. These disciplines were practices of the early church, demonstrating an inward disposition. Though we've only scratched the surface, it's clear that the disciplines should be a regular part, not only in the life of the Christian, but also that of the church. Spirituality, then, isn't merely about the individual, nor is it merely a private matter. What we do and who we are affects others. We're called to a life that's self-giving and other-centered, which stands in stark contrast to how most people in today's Western culture thinks about spirituality.

Theology and Building Character

In this chapter, we've explored the connection between theology and character. The Bible has much to say about character formation, but discussion on character in Scripture is always linked to sound theology. We especially see that the fruit of the Spirit and Christian virtue are grounded in God's own character. Lastly, theology plays a central part in helping us to understand what it means to be spiritual and to practice the disciplines. As we saw, being spiritual is connected to the kind of person that we're called to be, and it takes place in and through the power of the Holy Spirit working in us. Moreover, how we practice the disciplines should be taken into connection with our understanding of how they fit within the overall context of the Church (ecclesiology).

Chapter Eight

Making Disciples

Jesus' Commission

As we saw in chapter six, Jesus has called His followers to the task of making disciples. Making disciples is part of what we've been calling GC² (The Great Commandments and the Great Commission). But what we're going to concern ourselves with in the following pages is what making disciples looks like. What does it mean for Christians to make disciples? As we discuss disciple making, we'll need to consider other questions as well: What is the Gospel? How do we become disciples? What does theology have to do with disciple-making? It would be appropriate, then, to begin by briefly working through some key Great Commission passages.

There are many Great Commission passages we could include, but for our purposes we're only going to focus on three: Matthew 28:18-20; Luke 24:45-49; and Acts 1:8. Let's take each of these in order.

Matthew 28:18-20

[18] And Jesus came and said to them, "All authority in heaven and on earth has been given to me. [19] Go therefore and make disciples of all nations, baptizing them in the name of the Father and of the Son and of the Holy Spirit, [20] teaching them to observe all that I have commanded you. And behold, I am with you always, to the end of the age."

We've already discussed this passage briefly in chapter six, but now we're going to unpack it a bit more, breaking it down into its constituent parts.

Contextually, this passage, along with the following two Scriptures, takes place after Jesus' death and resurrection and just before His ascension. Like a general giving orders before going out to war, Jesus provides His disciples with their final instructions—"Go therefore and make disciples." But there's a vital ingredient to these instructions often overlooked, and its thrust is significantly theological. Jesus tells them that He's been given "[a]ll authority in heaven and on earth." The word "authority" used here usually means "power" and "authority" in the New Testament Greek, and it can carry with it the idea of a "ruling power."[1] The combination of "in heaven and on earth" tells us that Jesus' authority encompasses the entire created order. When Jesus speaks about having "authority," He means that He's been given complete dominion (rulership) and power over all things. No place is left untouched by Jesus' dominion, rule, and Lordship. We should take comfort in knowing that in sending us out, Jesus (to put it quite colloquially) has our backs! This should also give us great confidence. We are to engage in the task of disciple-making under Jesus' authority.

The central command of this passage isn't to "go," "baptize," or "teach"; rather, it's to "make disciples." Making disciples includes each of these elements. As we're going out into the world, we are to make disciples, which includes baptizing and teaching them. In baptizing them, Jesus' disciples are to do it "in the name of the Father and of the Son and of the Holy Spirit." This formula is Trinitarian in nature, demarcating the Christian God from all other pagan gods and deities. It shows identity. Those who are baptized in the name of the Father, Son, and Holy Spirit identify as followers of the one, true God, who is Triune and has been revealed most fully through the incarnate Son—the one who is now sending them out. What is it that they're to teach? To observe all that the Son has commanded. In other words, as Jesus' followers go out and make disciples, they're to model and imitate Jesus, instructing others on all that He taught and commanded. But the idea isn't merely a cognitive exercise. Disciple making includes teaching them to "observe" what Jesus taught. Disciples are to live out and put into practice what Jesus taught and commanded.

Lastly, Jesus emphasized to His disciples that they don't have to make disciples alone. Not only are we to make disciples in and through Jesus' power and authority, but He promises to be with us as we make disciples. How bold would we be if we took this to heart and task? What would our efforts at discipleship look like?

Luke 24:46-49

[45] Then he opened their minds to understand the Scriptures, [46] and said to them, "Thus it is written, that the Christ should suffer and on the third day rise from the dead, [47] and that repentance for the forgiveness of sins should be proclaimed in his name to all nations, beginning from Jerusalem. [48] You are witnesses of these things. [49] And behold, I am sending the promise of my Father upon you. But stay in the city until you are clothed with power from on high."

This passage from Luke is similar to the one from the Gospel of Matthew. There are, however, certain elements contained in this passage not found in the previous one.

First off, we see two things: Jesus opened their mind to understand the Scriptures and they are to be witnesses. It's important we keep in mind that Jesus is speaking specifically to those who witnessed His death and resurrection. What

---

[1]"*exousia*," in *The Lexham Analytic Lexicon to the Greek New Testament*, second revised ed. (Logos Bible Software, 2011).

we're to pass on to others is that which has been handed down to us through eye-witness testimony. What they received is through Jesus' direct teaching and what they've witnessed first-hand about Jesus.

Second, what we're to pass on to others has certain significant theological content. Key components include: "it is written," "Christ should suffer," "on the third day rise from the dead," and "repentance for the forgiveness of sins should be proclaimed to all nations." Why must we emphasize "it is written"? This is central. The events surrounding Jesus didn't take place in a religious, historical, and social vacuum. Jesus' death and resurrection took place within certain religious and historical circumstances. Jesus, as the anointed Messiah (the Christ), is the fulfillment of what God had been doing through Israel up to that point. When Jesus says, "it is written," He is referring to the fulfillment of prophecy about the Jewish Messiah who was to come. Furthermore, rather than being contrary to the Old Testament, what we find in the life and ministry of Jesus, and especially regarding the death and resurrection of Jesus, as reflected in the Gospels, is in alignment with the Jewish Scriptures. The content of fulfilled prophecy includes the Messiah's suffering, death and resurrection, and the offering of repentance and forgiveness of sins to all nations. These items should fill out the content of what we're proclaiming and teaching to others, as we make disciples. We should emphasize Jesus as the Messiah—Israel's anointed deliverer. Christ isn't Jesus' last name, as some have wrongly thought, but it's the Greek word for messiah. But Jesus isn't the Messiah for Israel only, but for the whole world (to all nations). The central thrust of the gospel message itself, as we'll see more fully below, is the death and resurrection of Jesus. The result is that through Jesus' death and resurrection all nations are now offered repentance and forgiveness of sins.

Third, and finally, this passage tells us that Jesus is sending to His disciples "the promise" of His Father. This is a reference to the Holy Spirit, who is "the promise" "received from the Father" (Acts 2:23). It is the Spirit who enables and empowers Jesus' followers to go out and do the work of making the disciples, as the next verse also suggests.

Acts 1:8

[8] But you will receive power when the Holy Spirit has come upon you, and you will be my witnesses in Jerusalem and in all Judea and Samaria, and to the end of the earth."

At this point, the disciples had not yet received the Holy Spirit, but with the coming of the Spirit they were to receive power to be Jesus' witnesses. Notice, the disciples weren't to sit idly by until the Spirit came, nor were they to limit the task of disciple-making to their immediate locality; rather, they were to take the gospel out to Judea, Samaria, and utter most parts of the world.

Implications

What implications can we draw from the above passages. First, what we're called to is making disciples. This task includes evangelism, but it's certainly not limited to that. We're called to train others to follow Christ. Not only should we model Christ-likeness to them, but we're to teach them to live out Christ's teachings. So, it's not merely about teaching them what to think, nor is merely a cognitive act. Following Christ involves the whole person—head, heart, and hands. As we'll see in the last chapter, we're all called to be red-hot worshipers of the Triune God.

Second, when we engage in the task of evangelism, we must remember that Christ's death and resurrection is at the center of our proclamation. Unfortunately, I've seen various gospel presentations emphasize Jesus' death on the cross for forgiveness of sins and repentance for sin, but not the resurrection. That's only half of the message. Jesus has also been raised from the dead. This is a crucial part of the Gospel, as we'll see below.

Third, Jesus wants disciples from all nations. Jesus the Messiah isn't just for the people of Israel, nor is He the Messiah for one ethnic group. He's the Messiah and savior of all people. As we engage in the discipleship process, we're to make disciples of all people and in all places.

Fourth, as we engage in the discipleship process, we're not alone. The Triune God, to whom we point all glory and honor, aids us in the task. Jesus promises that we do it by His authority. Moreover, He promises to be with us as we make disciples. Lastly, God has sent His Spirit to empower His people as they go out and make disciples of all nations.

Getting the Gospel Right

In the previous section, we focused on Jesus' commission to make disciples. Now we turn to the Gospel itself. In this section, we're going to explore the key components of the Gospel, while also examining a popular misconception about it.

In popular Christian worship music, we often hear that the cross was enough. But is it? The word *gospel* simply means "good news. Jesus' work on the cross is indeed "good news" for us and for all who believe. But the authors of the New Testament didn't leave their message of the good news at the cross. Central to the heart of the Christian proclamation, and the lynchpin of the Christian faith, is the bodily resurrection of Jesus from the dead. The cross only makes sense in light of Jesus' resurrection. As Ross Clifford and Philip Johnson emphasize, the resurrection of Jesus stood at the center of each of the speeches and sermons in the book of Acts. Consider the following comparison of topics in those sermons and speeches:

Resurrection (100%)

Death/suffering (88%)

OT fulfillment (88%)

Christ/Lord (63%)

Forgiveness (63%)

Repentance (50%)

Witness (50%)

Judgment (38%)[2]

We should be suspect of any Gospel presentation that doesn't include the bodily resurrection of Jesus.

Perhaps, at the heart of the issue stands a misunderstanding about the Gospel message. Darrell Bock rightly points out that too often Christians see the gospel as nothing more than a "transaction," the removal of a debt owed, and they often miss its fuller meaning.[3] Christ's work on the cross is central to the Gospel message (1 Corinthians 1:23; 15:3-5). It is at the core of the good news; however, we cannot leave it there:

> When Paul refers to the cross in this early part of 1 Corinthians, the term *cross* functions as the hub and a synecdoche for all that Jesus' work brings. A synecdoche is a part that represents the whole. I mention one central thing to picture all of it. For example, if I speak of the Law and the Prophets, I am speaking of the whole Old Testament. If I speak of fifty head of cattle, I'm talking about fifty whole cows—heads, hooves, bodies, and tails—not just fifty heads. Likewise, when Paul speaks of the cross here [in 1 Corinthians 1:23], he is using the word as a synecdoche for the whole of the gospel.[4]

The Gospel, suggests Bock, began with a promise of new life, which is brought about through the giving of the promised Holy Spirit. It starts with God's covenant with Abraham and continues up through the Davidic and New Covenants.[5]

God promised Abraham that He would be the father of a great nation and that all the nations of the world would be blessed through Him (Gen 12:1-3). In His covenant with David, God promised Israel's greatest king an ancestor who would rule on his throne with an everlasting reign. In the New Covenant, God promises renewal for His people (Jer 31:31-34). We find similar language in the book of Ezekiel. God promises to "clean" His people from all their "uncleanliness," put within them "a new heart" and "a new spirit," remove their "heart of stone," and give them a "heart of flesh" (Ezek 36:25-28). God's renewal comes in two ways:

---

[2]Ross Clifford and Philip Johnson, *The Cross Is Not Enough: Living as Witnesses to the Resurrection* (Grand Rapids, MI: Baker Books, 2012).

[3]Darrell L. Bock, *Recovering the Real Lost Gospel: Reclaiming the Gospel as Good News* (Nashville, TN: Broadman and Holman, 2010), 2.

[4]Ibid., 4.

[5]Ibid., 10.

through cleansing His people of their sin and through putting within them the promised Holy Spirit.[6]

This promise of the cleansing of sins and the coming of the Holy Spirit is what we see fulfilled through the finished work of Jesus in the Gospels and the book of Acts. Through Christ's cross comes the cleansing and the forgiveness of sins; through the resurrection comes the giving of new life through the sending of and empowerment by the Holy Spirit. Both themes (i.e., the forgiveness of sins and the sending of the Holy Spirit), as found in connection to Jesus' resurrection, dominate the book of Acts. In Acts 1:8, Jesus commands the disciples to remain in Jerusalem until they receive the Holy Spirit, which takes place on the day of Pentecost (Acts 2:1-13), fulfilling the prophecy in Joel 2:28-32 that God would "pour out" His "Spirit on all flesh" (Acts 2:17). This same Spirit is later given to the Gentiles (Acts 10:47; 15:7-8). Moreover, the first gospel message in the book of Acts, suggests Bock, included the forgiveness of sins and *"the reception of the Spirit of God, the reception of a promise God had made to enable His people."*[7]

Finally, the effects of the gospel are not limited to human redemption, but stretches to all of creation. Consider Paul's words in his letter the Colossians:

> [19] For in him all the fullness of God was pleased to dwell, [20] and through him to reconcile to himself all things, whether on earth or in heaven, making peace by the blood of his cross. (Col 1:19-20)

Similarly, Paul writes to the Christians in Rome:

> [19] For the creation waits with eager longing for the revealing of the sons of God. [20] For the creation was subjected to futility, not willingly, but because of him who subjected it, in hope [21] that the creation itself will be set free from its bondage to corruption and obtain the freedom of the glory of the children of God. [22] For we know that the whole creation has been groaning together in the pains of childbirth until now. [23] And not only the creation, but we ourselves, who have the firstfruits of the Spirit, groan inwardly as we wait eagerly for adoption as sons, the redemption of our bodies. (Rom 8:19-23)

Here, Paul links creation's liberation "from its bondage to corruption" with the redemption of our bodies. God, through the work of Christ and by the renewal of the Spirit, is in the process of reversing the effects of the Fall, which has ramifications, not only for humanity, but for all of creation.

Becoming a Disciple

Having considered the Gospel, what, then, does it mean to become a disciple? Dallas Willard is correct in stressing that one can know a lot about Jesus and not be His disciple.[8] The same is true for those who study theology. Just because a

---

[6]Ibid., 7-12.

[7]Ibid., 17. [Emphasis his]

[8]Dallas Willard, *The Divine Conspiracy: Rediscovering Our Hidden Life in God* (New York: HarperOne, 1997), 291.

person studies theology doesn't mean he or she's a follower of Jesus. Nevertheless, we shouldn't take that to mean that theology is unimportant. Theology is crucial, as this book has already pointed out in so many ways. The content of our faith matters. Consider the words of philosopher J. P. Moreland: "the actual content of what we believe about God, morality, politics, life after death, and so on will shape the contours of our life and actions."[9] He continues, "In fact, the contents of our beliefs are so important that according to Scripture, our eternal destiny is determined by what we believe about Jesus Christ."[10]

How, then, are we to become disciples of Jesus Christ? Willard provides three steps: ask, dwell, and decide.[11] First, we should continually *ask* Jesus to show himself to us "more fully." Not only as we see Him represented in the Gospels, but as He is now, the divine Creator of all things who holds the universe together. Sometimes, this may require devoting quiet time alone with God, writing down our thoughts and prayers. Second, we should *dwell* in God's word. On this point, Willard writes:

> But dwelling in his word is not just intensive and continuous study of the Gospels, though it is that. It is also putting them into practice. To dwell in his word we must know it; know what it is and what it means. But we really *dwell* in it by putting it into practice. Of course, we shall do so very imperfectly at first. At that point we have perhaps not even come to be a committed disciple. We are only thinking about how to become one. Nevertheless, we can count on Jesus to meet us in our admittedly imperfect efforts to put his word into practice. Where his word is, there he is. He does not leave his words to stand alone in the world. And his loveliness and strength will certainly be personally revealed to those who will simply make the effort to do what his words indicate.[12]

This, however, takes effort. We can also look seriously into the lives of other Christians who have gone on before us, especially those "who truly have apprenticed themselves to him [Jesus]."[13] On this point, however, Willard warns that we should soak ourselves in the Gospels before turning to the lives of others. Lastly, we should seek out groups of Jesus' followers, people who have dedicated themselves to apprentice after Jesus. The third and last step is to *decide*. Often, we fail at discipleship because we simply don't commit ourselves to becoming apprentices of Jesus.[14]

Theology and Discipleship

Christ gave His followers the task of going into all the world to make disciples. This chapter argued that making disciples includes, not only doing evangelism,

---

[9]J. P. Moreland, *Kingdom Triangle: Recover the Christian Mind, Renovate the Soul, Restore the Spirit's Power* (Grand Rapids, MI: Zondervan, 2007), 131.

[10]Ibid.

[11]Willard, *The Divine Conspiracy*, 295-298.

[12]Ibid., 296.

[13]Ibid., 297.

[14]Ibid., 297-299.

but teaching others all that Jesus commanded, which means we must have a good handle on Christian doctrine. Believers are to pass on the faith handed down to us by Jesus and the apostles (Jud 3). All that we do should be for the edification and building up of the church.

Chapter Nine

Growing in Worship

Defining Worship

One of the core tenets of evangelicalism is its zeal and passion for reaching the lost. The word evangelical comes from the Greek work *euaggelion,* which means "gospel" or "good news." Evangelicals, on the whole, have dedicated themselves to fulfilling the Great Commission, following Jesus' call to make discipleship of all nations. Evangelism and missions are placed as a top priority among many evangelical churches. As important as evangelism and missions are, they should be driven by something greater—our zeal and passion for God.

As hard as it is for some to accept, missions and evangelism are not our ultimate concern. Notice the world 'ultimate' here. Ultimate refers to that which is most significant or important. The most important concern for a Christian should be to find our joy, pleasure, and hope in God and not in other things. Pastor John Piper insightfully makes this point in his book, *Let the Nations Be Glad*:

> Missions is not the ultimate goal of the church. Worship is. Missions exists because worship doesn't. Worship is ultimate, not missions, because God is ultimate, not man. When this age is over, and the countless millions of the redeemed fall on their faces before the throne of God, missions will be no more. It is a temporary necessity. But worship abides forever . . . . Worship, therefore, is the fuel and goal of missions. It's the goal of missions because in missions we simply aim to bring the nations into the white-hot enjoyment of God's glory. The goal of missions is the gladness of the peoples in the greatness of God.[1]

Furthermore, as we reflect on the ultimacy of worship, the purpose of missions and evangelism isn't merely about "getting people saved," though it certainly includes that. Moreover, the Christian life does not end with salvation and forgiveness of sin. Unfortunately, for many of us, that's as far as we've taken it. As followers of the Triune God, we are called to be a light to the nations, a city on the hill that is to be noticed by all who pass by or who are looking from far off. But what is it that the lost ought to see? The lost should see a people of God sold

---

[1]John Piper, *Let the Nations Be Glad: The Supremacy of God in Missions,* 2nd ed. (Grand Rapids, MI; Baker Academic, 2003), 17.

out for Him, and for Him alone! As Piper rightly claims above, worship, as "the fuel and goal of missions," is to bring "the nations into the white-hot enjoyment of God's glory." The goal of missions and evangelism is to point all people to the greatness of our God.

If you recall from chapter six, a significant part of the Christian life revolves around GC². First in order, however, are the Great Commandments:

> "The most important is, 'Hear, O Israel: The Lord our God, the Lord is one. [30] And you shall love the Lord your God with all your heart and with all your soul and with all your mind and with all your strength.' [31] The second is this: 'You shall love your neighbor as yourself.' There is no other commandment greater than these." (Mk 12:29-31)

Notice the order—God first, then our neighbors. Worship begins with a vertical relationship toward God and not with a horizontal one toward our fellow humans. That's not to say that horizontal relationships are unimportant. They certainly are. As the Elder John tells us, our love for others serves as a barometer for our love for God (1 Jn 4:7-8). Jesus' point, in giving the Greatest Commandment, is that everything about us should be geared toward loving God supremely. We are to love God with every ounce of our being. Loving God is central to worship.

Often, we limit worship to singing songs, giving of our tithes and offerings, and listening to the pastor's sermon. These kinds of activities certainly can be a part of our worship, but worship can't be limited to an activity. Nor can it be limited to a place. For the Christian, worship happens daily. Worship happens moment by moment. We are to take every thought captive. We are to be consumed by our great God. We might define the act of Christian worship as follows: *Worship is having an all-encompassing or consuming zeal and passion for God, in whom we find ultimate joy and delight and a desire that cannot be quenched because of His infinite greatness.*

Worship is not merely an outward way of life; rather, it begins internally. Those things which are outward ought to reflect that which has taken place internally. As we reflect on the nature of worship, it would do us well to hear Jesus' words to the woman at the well:

> Jesus said to her, "Woman, believe me, the hour is coming when neither on this mountain nor in Jerusalem will you worship the Father. [22] You worship what you do not know; we worship what we know, for salvation is from the Jews. [23] But the hour is coming, and is now here, when the true worshipers will worship the Father in spirit and truth, for the Father is seeking such people to worship him. [24] God is spirit, and those who worship him must worship in spirit and truth." (Jn 4:21-24)

Worship of God is not limited by boundaries or location. There is no one place where we are to worship God. Why is that? God is spirit. He is not bound to anyplace in our four-dimensional space-time universe. God transcends all created reality. As Paul tells the Epicureans and Stoics in His speech on Mars Hill, "The God who made the world and everything in it, being Lord of heaven and earth, does not live in temples made by man, . . . he himself gives to all mankind life and breath and everything" (Acts 17:24-25). Or, as the Lord proclaims through Isaiah the prophet:

> Heaven is my throne,
>
> and the earth is my footstool;
>
> what is the house that you would build for me,
>
> and what is the place of my rest?
>
> ²All these things my hand has made,
>
> and so all these things came to be,
>
> declares the LORD. (Is 66:1)

Moreover, God is omnipresent (Ps 139:7-18)—present to all places and all times—and He's omniscient (all-knowing), knowing what's in our hearts and our minds (Jer 12:3; 1 Chr 29:17; Ps 139:1-2; Acts 15:8). What God looks for in a worshiper is someone "who is humble and contrite in spirit and trembles" at His word (Is 66:2). Worship of God, then, is a disposition. It's a way of life and an attitude, which is grounded in the truth of who God is and His desire for us to be in a proper relationship with Him.

Avoiding Idols

What is it that most occupies our thoughts and desires? Our answer to that question speaks volumes to what's ultimate in our lives.

For many of us Christians, we practice syncretism. A syncretist is someone who fuses together beliefs from differing and/or contradictory belief systems. One of the reasons Christians stumble into syncretism is because they are often not aware of what it is that that they're mixing into their worldview. These ideologies often keep us from desiring and being passionate for the Lord. Consider the following ideologies Christians often buy into without realizing that they're doing it:

Materialism – We become materialists when we're not satisfied with what we have. We are constantly wanting more, whether it's the latest gadget or to have the best look in order to fit in with others. For many of us, we seek happiness in material things. Scripture teaches that we're not to put our hope in things; rather, we should find our hope in God, who takes care of our needs (Mt 6:25-34; Phil 4:10-13)

Hedonism – We become hedonists when we live for now, as if life has no eternal value or consequences. We find pleasure in anything or everything other than God. But what we do in this life does matter. There is eternal value in the things we do on this earth, and there is more to life than living for pleasure (Lk 12:23; 1 Cor 3:5-17).

Individualism – We fall into individualism when we begin thinking life revolves mostly around me and what I want. Some of us are so worried about being authentic or unique that such pursuits become our ultimate concern. As Christians, we are called to love God and to love others *as ourselves* (Mk 12:29-31). Our attitude should be like Jesus', who was in His very nature God, but nevertheless emptied Himself, taking on the form of a servant (Phil 2:6-18).

Emotionalism – We adhere to emotionalism when we allow our emotions or subjective feelings to rule over what we believe about God and His promises toward us. Spiritual decisions are made based on what we feel to be true. While emotions are good and God-given, we must be careful not to allow them to dictate to us what's true; rather, truth is grounded objectively in Christ and reflected in God's revelation to us (Jn 8:32; 16:13; 17:17; 1 Cor 14:33; Eph 4:17-24; Col 2:3; 1 Tim 3:16; 2 Pt 1:21;Jud 3)

We can sum up the above "isms" in one word—"idolatry." In the book of Isaiah, the prophet paints a picture of the foolishness of idolatry:

[12] The ironsmith takes a cutting tool and works it over the coals. He fashions it with hammers and works it with his strong arm. He becomes hungry, and his strength fails; he drinks no water and is faint. [13] The carpenter stretches a line; he marks it out with a pencil. He shapes it with planes and marks it with a compass. He shapes it into the figure of a man, with the beauty of a man, to dwell in a house. [14] He cuts down cedars, or he chooses a cypress tree or an oak and lets it grow strong among the trees of the forest. He plants a cedar and the rain nourishes it. [15] Then it becomes fuel for a man. He takes a part of it and warms himself; he kindles a fire and bakes bread. Also he makes a god and worships it; he makes it an idol and falls down before it. [16] Half of it he burns in the fire. Over the half he eats meat; he roasts it and is satisfied. Also he warms himself and says, "Aha, I am warm, I have seen the fire!" [17] And the rest of it he makes into a god, his idol, and falls down to it and worships it. He prays to it and says, "Deliver me, for you are my god!"

[18] They know not, nor do they discern, for he has shut their eyes, so that they cannot see, and their hearts, so that they cannot understand. [19] No one considers, nor is there knowledge or discernment to say, "Half of it I burned in the fire; I also baked bread on its coals; I roasted meat and have eaten. And shall I make the rest of it an abomination? Shall I fall down before a block of wood?" [20] He feeds on ashes; a deluded heart has led him astray, and he cannot deliver himself or say, "Is there not a lie in my right hand?" (Is 44:12-20)

Unfortunately, as Christians we are often much like the foolish man who fashions an idol. We incorporate these ideologies into our Christian worldview without realizing that we're doing it. We get caught up in hedonism or materialism and we become blinded by these things that stand in our way from finding sole pleasure and hope in the triune God. To what extent are we like the idolater where we cannot even ask ourselves "[i]s there not a lie in my right hand?" It's imperative that we examine our hearts, searching to find if there is some form of idolatry that's keeping us from being satisfied in the Lord.

What's tragic is that for many of us we know more about our cell phones and how they work than we know about our God and Creator. We can talk all day long about the best football team, what's going on in politics, or what the stock market is doing, but we cannot describe what Scripture teaches about God. We're knowledgeable and thrive on understanding about things that have no ultimate significance, but fail to understand what matters most. We've made created things into our gods and we have molded them into our likeness and image. Consider Paul's words in his letter to the Romans:

> For although they knew God, they did not honor him as God or give thanks to him, but they became futile in their thinking, and their foolish hearts were darkened. [22] Claiming to be wise, they became fools, [23] and exchanged the glory of the immortal God for images resembling mortal man and birds and animals and creeping things.

> [24] Therefore God gave them up in the lusts of their hearts to impurity, to the dishonoring of their bodies among themselves, [25] because they exchanged the truth about God for a lie and worshiped and served the creature rather than the Creator, who is blessed forever! Amen. (Romans 1:21-25)

Paul is speaking here of the unregenerate person. However, how often do we Christians do the same thing. How often do we turn our hearts and affections away from God?

God has created us to worship and to have fellowship with Him, but sin separates us from God and His good purposes, as A. W. Tozer reminds us:

> God formed us for His pleasure, and so formed us that we, as well as He, can, in divine communion, enjoy the sweet and mysterious mingling of kindred personalities. He meant us to see Him and live with Him and draw our life from His smile. But we have been guilty of that "foul revolt" of which Milton speaks when describing the rebellion of Satan and his hosts. We have broken with God. We have ceased to obey Him or love Him, and in guilt and fear have fled as far as possible from His presence.[2]

In his book, *Pleasure Evermore*, theologian Sam Storm describes sin as what we do when we don't find our ultimate satisfaction in God. He suggests that the key to victorious living as Christians and in overcoming sin in our lives is through finding satisfaction "with all that God is for us in Jesus."[3] He continues, "the only way to fight the seductive power of one pleasure is with a greater pleasure, a more pleasing pleasure, the pleasure that comes from falling in love with Jesus. . . . God is most glorified in us when we are most happy and delighted and satisfied in Him."[4] God should be the sole ruler in our lives, not sin. We should desire Him above all other things.

Psalm 24:1-2 tells us that the earth belongs to the LORD and all that's within it—including God's human creatures. Our lives, all that we do and all that we

---

[2]A. W. Tozer, *The Pursuit of God*, quoted in *Tozer on Worship an Entertainment*, compiled by James L. Snyder (Camp Hill, PA: WingSpreadPublishers, 1997), 77.

[3]Sam Storms, *Pleasure Evermore: The Life-Changing Power of Enjoying God* (Colorado Springs, CO: NavPress, 2000), 27.

[4]Ibid., 27-28.

have, belong to the Lord. We're to give everything over to the Lordship of Christ. Work, family, school, possessions, thoughts, attitudes—all belong to the Lord. Having God front-and-center in our lives, recognizing that He is the Lord over all, overflows into a life of flourishing, affecting how we interact with and engage others.

Theology and Worship

As Christians, what then is the primary role of theology? Theology helps us to center and refocus our thoughts on God, the one who matters most. It shows us our proper place in the created order. God is God and we are not. We are creatures, owing our very existence to the Creator. Moreover, theology helps us to see our need for salvation and how Great our God is in offering forgiveness, hope, and redemption. Theology leads to a life of thankfulness to our God for His goodness and great deeds towards us. The primary function of theology, if done properly, leads to a life of worship!

Chapter Ten

Integrating Faith

Integration of Faith and Learning

So far, we've seen that theology is important in shaping our worldviews, defending the faith, correcting false teaching, removing doubt, transforming our minds, building character, making disciples, and growing in worship. As emphasized in chapter one, everything is essentially theological. Everything in life boils down to a theological question. Our actions, beliefs, and attitudes are all influenced by our theological perspectives. In what follows, we're going to conclude our journey by focusing on how to integrate faith into our lives. We're going to do this in two ways. First, we'll consider certain biblical principles that guide and shape how we live in our various spheres of influence—family, work, and play. Second, we'll focus on ways of analyzing and engaging the arts and culture. But before moving on to each of these, we'll take some space to consider just what we mean by "integration."

Mark Eckel, in his book, *The Whole Truth*, suggests that people often wrongly confuse biblical integration with illustration, character quality instruction, spiritualization, transmission, correlation, application, evangelization, or personification. Instead, suggests Eckel, biblical integration centers on the concept of permeation.[1] What he means by this is that whatever is being studied, "biblical principles should permeate everything."[2] Biblical integration provides us with a sense of "wholeness," "synthesis," or "completion."[3] He continues, "[t]eachers need to recover God-centered thought patterns that invigorate every discipline."[4] Though aimed at Christian educator's, Eckel's emphasis on "God-centered thought patterns" is spot on and applies to all believers. Biblical principles should soak every square inch of how we Christians think about our disciplines and chosen vocations.

---

[1] Mark Eckel, *The Whole Truth: Classroom Strategies for Biblical Integration* (Xulon Press, 2003), 65-73.

[2] Ibid., 73.

[3] Ibid.

[4] Ibid.

In a similar vein, Mark Cosgrove suggests that faith and learning integration "means the relating of one's biblical worldview to the learning that is taking place in the academic or cultural arenas."[5] Most often discussion on faith and learning integration takes place within the Christian university or Bible College. But Cosgrove is correct in pointing out that it should not be limited only to academic arenas, especially because learning takes place beyond the academic context. As Christians, learning should be a vital part of both family and church life. Moreover, our worldviews impact how we think about every area of life. The integration of faith and learning isn't a one-time process, but requires continual analysis of how our faith impacts the various arenas of life.

Cosgrove suggests three ways that the integration of faith and learning is important to the Christian life. First, integration serves as a filter in our thinking. It can aid us in evaluating truth claims. For example, if evolutionary scientists suggest that human beings are just one species among others, and that we should not place humans above other animals, we see an immediate conflict with the Christian worldview, which tells us that humans were made in the image and likeness of God—something that cannot be said about God's other earthly creatures.[6] Second, integration can affect how we think and act. Consider his words on this point:

> The Christian worldview is not a static creed that we memorize but a living belief system that we enter into with our whole lives. Christianity is a living relationship with our Creator. This relationship affects us in ways that can change how we function as scholars, musicians, politicians, and parents. Christian maturation can relate to the work of a person in various ways. The Christian who is growing in Christlike compassion might spend more time and resources in the study of the family or of alcoholism, rather than in academic or cultural areas more current in the mind of the world.[7]

Third, and lastly, integration functions as a two-way street in our growth process. Our faith affects our learning as much as our learning affects our faith. Not only does our faith serve as a filter for our thinking, but it also can aid us in developing better ways of thinking about our academic disciplines, culture, and other spheres of influence in which we live, move, and have our being. Yet, on the other hand, learning may also affect our faith in various ways. "Some of the learning that affects our faith development comes from Bible teaching," suggests Cosgrove, "but some also can come from more ordinary learning."[8] He continues, "[k]nowledge of grammar, logic, history, and current events often make Scripture come alive to us."[9]

---

[5]Mark P. Cosgrove, *Foundations of Christian Thought: Faith, Learning, and the Christian Worldview* (Grand Rapids, MI: Kregel, 2006), 54.

[6]Ibid., 59-60.

[7]Ibid., 60.

[8]Ibid., 61.

[9]Ibid.

What Cosgrove (and Eckel, too) is getting at here, goes back to our discussion in chapter one on the two books of revelation—Scripture and the world. If truth is to be found in the world, whether in the pages of Scripture or in the world, it is ultimately grounded in Christ, who is the source of all truth. Truth, then, is ultimately unitary, but because of sin, we often only see things partially and frag- mented. That's why when we analyze and seek to understand God's good world, we must view it in light of God's special revelation to us, as found within the pages of Scripture. God's special revelation becomes the lens by which we view and understand the world. To put it another way, Scripture brings cohesiveness and coherence to what we discover through the exploration of God's good world. Through integration, our ultimate goal is to discover truth and to see things how God intended them.

Biblical Principles for Integration

Now that we have a better understanding on what integration is, let us focus our attention on the "how" of biblical integration. While many others could be given, in what follows, we'll consider eight key biblical principles for integration that can be applied to various arenas of life.

Principle #1: The Lordship of God in Our Lives

As we dive into the various principles, the first to consider is God's Lordship over all things. Ultimately, everything belongs to the Lord, because He is the Sovereign Creator of all things (Gen 1:1; Neh 9:6; Is 42:5; 66:2; Jn 1:1-3; 1 Cor 8:6; Col 1:16; Heb 1:2; 11:3; Rev 4:11). As the psalmist declares:

[1] The earth is the Lord's and the fullness hereof, the world and those who dwell therein,
[2] for he has founded it upon the seas

and established it upon the rivers. (Psalm 24:1-2

As Christians, we are to give all that we are, all that we do, and all that we have over to the Lordship of Christ, who is Himself God incarnate (Jn 1:14; Phil 2:7-8). The Lordship of Christ applies to all areas of life, even to our disciplines of study, vocations, and play. Let me be clear, giving our lives over to the Lordship of Christ doesn't mean we have no freedom in our choices. God certainly does give us significant freedom in our daily lives. But what this means is that as we're pursuing a discipline or vocation, we are to take our thoughts captive for Christ (2 Cor 10:6) in our studies and in our learning, and we are to do our work as if we're doing it unto the Lord (Col 3:23).

Now, you might be wondering: "if God gives us freedom, how are we to discern God's will for our lives?" In his little book, *Found: God's Will*, pastor John MacArthur gives some great advice on discerning God's will. "God's will," says MacArthur, "is that you be saved, Spirit-filled, sanctified, submissive, and suffering."[10] He continues, "If you are doing all five of the basic things, do you know what the next principle of God's will is? Do whatever you want!"[11] If MacArthur is right, it's encouraging to know that God's will centers more on whether we're being obedient and submissive to Him, growing in our faith, and living a life that's willing to serve Jesus with all that we have, than on what we're doing.

Principle #2: All Truth is God's Truth

Scripture tells us that God is the Creator of all things and that Christ is the source and ground of all knowledge and wisdom (Gen 1; Ps 24:1-2; Is 28:23-26; Jn 1:1-3; Col 1:16; 2:8; Heb 1:2-3). If truth is to be found in the world, then such truth is ultimately grounded in the infinite, all-knowing, and wise Creator who made all things. As theologian Louis Berkhof reminds us, God "is the source of all truth, not only in the sphere of morals and religion, but also in every field of scientific endeavor."[12] God, as the infinite and wise Creator, has structured the world in such a way that it can be known and understood. Moreover, as creatures who are made in the image and likeness of God (Gen 1:26-27), God has made us in such a way that we can know and understand His world. Take, for example, the farmer. Isaiah the prophet tells us that God, who "is wonderful in counsel and excellent in wisdom," is the one who instructs the farmer on how to plant, harvest, and make grain (Is 28:23-29).

Principle #3: Creation, Fall, Redemption

God created all things good (Gen 1:4, 9, 12, 18, 21, 25, 31); however, God's good creation was soon distorted by humanity's rebellion (sin) against Him. This act of rebellion against God is known as the Fall. The Fall brought with it various consequences. Not only did the Fall result in separation from God, but it also brought death, disease, and destruction to all human spheres of life and influence. Despite the Fall, God is seeking and working to redeem and restore His creatures and the created order (Rom 8:18-25; Col 1:19-20).

---

[10]John MacArthur, Jr., *Found: God's Will: Find the Direction and Purpose God Wants for Your Life*, rev. ed. (Colorado Springs, CO: Victor, 1977), 54. It would be helpful to clarify what MacArthur means by "suffering." He doesn't mean that we should become masochists, seeking out opportunities to suffer. Rather, what he has in mind is that we be willing to suffer for the cause of Christ. What that might look like is giving up our favorite coffee drink once a week in order to sponsor a child monthly through a Christian organization like Compassion International. Or, it may look like giving up our time in order to serve the homeless.

[11]Ibid.

[12]Louis Berkhof, *Systematic Theology*, new combined ed. (Grand Rapids, MI: Wm. B. Eerdmans Publishing Co., 1996), 69.

Principle #4: The Cultural Mandate

God gave humans the task of being vice-regents over the earth. They were to populate, subdue, and have dominion over it (Gen 1:28-29). Albert Wolters provides a helpful perspective on the significance of the cultural mandate.

> The creation mandate provides a sort of climax to the six days of creation. The stage with all its rich variety of props has been set by the stage director, the actors are introduced, and as the curtain raises and the stage director moves backstage, they are given their opening cue. The drama of human history is about to begin, and the first and foundational Word of God to his children is the command to "fill and subdue."[13]

God didn't create the world to be a static entity; rather, he created the world to be filled out, so to speak. God's human creatures were to be a part of "the ongoing creational work of God, to be God's helper in executing to the end the blueprint for his masterpiece."[14]

Principle #5: The Imago Dei

Humans were made in the image and likeness of God (Gen 1:26-27; 9:6; Ps 8; Js 3:9). The *imago Dei* is the ground for human rights and human responsibility toward one another. People should be treated with respect and dignity because they were made in the image and likeness of God. Such rights are endowed by their Creator; yet, with such rights, humans have responsibility and must be held accountable for their actions (Gen 1:26-27; 2; 9:6; Ps 8; Ex 20-22; Lv 19; Dt 20-25; Js 2:1-13; 3:9).

Principle #6: In the World, Not of the World

Christians are not to isolate themselves into a sub-culture, nor are they to "conform to the pattern of this world" (Rom 12:2); rather, they are to be in the world, but not be of the world (Mt 5:3-16; Lk 15; Acts 17:22-36; Rom 12:1-2; 1 Pt 3:13-17). A great example of this is found in the Babylonian captives (e.g., Daniel) that were encouraged by the prophet Jeremiah to live and prosper in the city. They were to be a light and an example in the midst of pagan Babylon (Jer 29:4-9).

Principle #7: God's Attributes as a Source for Integration

This is not so much a singular principle as much as it's a cluster of principles grounded in God's divine attributes. As we reflect on God's character and nature, various principles for integration emerge, especially in connection to the imago

---

[13] Albert M. Wolters, *Creation Regained: Biblical Basics for a Reformational Worldview*, second edition (Grand Rapids, MI: Wm. B. Eerdmans Publishing Co., 2005), 43.
[14] Ibid., 44.

Dei. A whole book could be written on this topic alone, but for our purposes, we'll only consider some key areas.

Creator/creature distinction – We humans are created, contingent beings. We owe our very existence to God, who is eternal and infinite. The Creator/creature distinction reminds us that we are finite and limited in our natures. Understanding our place within the created order brings about a life of humility, awe, and thankfulness for our very existence.

Omnipotence – God alone is all-powerful. Though we are not, as His image-bearers, God has created us with the capacity to not only have intentions, but to carry out those intentions through various actions. It is because of this ability to act and to carry out our intentions in this world that we can pursue our vocations, get caught up in play, and accomplish our goals and tasks.

Omniscience – Though we are limited in knowledge, we have been created in such a way that we reflect the divine Creator in our ability to know and understand God's good creation. Moreover, in learning, we use certain tools, such as logic and rhetoric, which reflect God's order in creation.[15] It's because of our ability to know, understand, and learn that we can explore our world through the sciences, seek wisdom through philosophy, and find ways to better our world through engineering.

Creator – We do not have the ability to create *ex nihilo* (out of nothing); however, as divine image bearers, we have been given the capacity to create, build, and design. Just as God evaluated and enjoyed His creation, we can evaluate and appreciate our creative works (Gen 1:4, 9, 12, 18, 21, 25, 31). The practice and study of art and music have their basis in the creativity of our Creator.

Holiness – As Christians, we are to be set apart because God is Himself set apart and Holy (Lev 11:44-45; 1 Pt 1:15-16). God's holiness is the basis for our own distinctive Christian living and thinking.[16]

Justice – We should pursue justice in the various areas of our lives and in our dealings with other people, whether in our work and vocation choices, in our play, or within society, since God is Himself just. It's because of God's justice that there is a place for law, government, and political science, especially in a world that has been infested by sin and corruption.

Goodness and Beauty – We should pursue goodness and beauty, since all earthly goods and beauty are derivate from God, the transcendent source of all that's good and beautify (Ps 27:4; 95:6; Js 1:17).

---

[15]Eckel, *The Whole Truth*, 114.
[16]Ibid.

Principle #8: No Distinction Between Sacred and Secular

Before moving on, it would be helpful to consider one last principle, which some might consider controversial—there is no distinction between the sacred and secular, at least in how most Christians think of it. As we work through this principle, it should become clearer why it's important for integration. In many ways, it culminates much of what we've discussed already, both in this chapter and in chapter one. Furthermore, it sets the stage for what we'll discuss in the following section.

How often do we hear people say things like, "don't watch that movie, it's secular" or "Christians should only listen to Christian music" or "the study of psychology is worldly"? But where do we draw the lines between what is sacred and what is secular? How do we determine whether something is worldly or sacred? Albert Wolters accurately pinpoints the problem:

> Christians of virtually every persuasion have tended to understand "world" to refer to a delimited area of the created order, an area that is usually called "worldly" or "secular" (from *saeculum*, the Latin rendering *aiōn*), which includes such fields as art, politics, scholarship (excluding theology), journalism, sports, business, and so on. In fact, to this way of thinking, the "world" includes everything outside the realm of the "sacred," which consists basically of the church, personal piety, and "sacred theology." Creation is therefore divided up neatly (although the dividing line may be defined differently by different Christians) into two realms: the secular and the sacred.[17]

Such compartmentalization, suggests Wolters, implies that there's no "worldliness" in our churches or that there can be holiness in various fields, such as art or business. That kind of thinking is more Gnostic than Christian, since it limits the sacred only to certain parts of creation.

Part of the problem lies in how people think of the word "worldliness". The Bible uses the word "world" in a variety of ways. Sometimes, it means the physical world in which we live (Rom 1:8). Other times, however, it refers to, in the words of Wolters, "the rottenness of the earth, the antithesis of creational goodness,"[18] as indicated in verses such as John 18:36, Romans 12:2, Colossians 2:8, James 1:27, and 2 Peter 2:20. Worldliness has to do more with the corruption of God's good world, and less about the actual physical reality that we live in.

We must remember that God created the earth and it belongs to Him: "For the earth is the Lords, and the fullness thereof" (Ps 24:1; 1 Cor 10:26). Moreover, all that God created was good, including physical and non-physical things. The problem lies in the fact that God's good creation has been corrupted and tainted by sin. Thus, there is nothing neutral. The first musical instruments were created by pagans (Gen 4:21), and yet these same instruments are used to worship God (Ps 150:3-4). We often claim that the Lord's work as being professions such as evangelist, missionary, or pastor; however, the first person mentioned in Scripture

---

[17]Wolters, *Creation Regained*, 64.
[18]Ibid.

to be filled with the Holy Spirit was Bezaleel—an artist and craftsman (Ex 31:3). Unfortunately, too often we overlook the fact that God appreciated what He created (Gen 1:4, 10, 12, 18, 21, 25, 31). Not only did God claim that His creation was good, but in Genesis 2:9 we're told that "God made to spring up every tree that is pleasant to the sight and good for food." As those made in the image and likeness of God, when we create and appreciate what we make, we ultimately reflect our good Creator.

How then are we to navigate our thinking on this? If you'll recall from chapter one, Wolters provides a helpful framework by making a distinction between "structure" and "direction." "[S]tructure," suggests Wolters, "denotes the 'essence' of a creaturely thing, the kind of creature it is by virtue of God's creational law."[19] In other words, structure refers to a thing's nature or essence, including all of the capacities and qualities that make it what it is. Rocks, dogs, elephants, and humans all have a certain structure to them. But this also applies to other created things, such as government, sex, and the earth. God established these things as part of His created order. The question, then, isn't whether such things are "good" or not; rather, the question is how have these good things been corrupted by sin. That's where direction comes in. On this, Wolters provides some helpful insight:

> Direction . . . designates the order of sin and redemption, the distortion of perversion of creation through the fall on the one hand and the redemption and restoration of creation in Christ on the other. Anything in creation can be directed either toward or away from God—that is, directed either in obedience or disobedience to his law. This double direction applies not only to individual human beings but also to such cultural phenomena as technology, art, and scholarship, to such societal institutions as labor unions, schools, and corporations, and to such human functions as emotionality, sexuality, and rationality. To the degree that these realities fail to live up to God's creational design for them, they are misdirected, abnormal, distorted. To the degree that they still conform to God's design, they are in the grip of a countervailing force that curbs or counteracts the distortion. Direction therefore always involves two tendencies moving either for or against God.[20]

To flesh this out, take, for example, sex. Sex is a good thing established by God, not merely for procreation, but also for enjoyment between a husband and a wife. But this good gift from God has been distorted by sin. Polygamy, prostitution, sex trafficking, homosexuality, adultery, and incest are all ways in which God's design plan for sex has been distorted.

As we think on "structure" and "direction," there are three questions we can ask on the task of integration: (1) What was God's intention in creating the thing in question?; (2) How has sin distorted it?; and (3) How can we be a part in what God is doing to redeem, restore, or reconcile it to Himself?

---

[19]Ibid., 89.
[20]Ibid., 59.

Analyzing and Engaging
the Arts and Culture

The list of principles above is by no means exhaustive. Many others could have been considered, but hopefully these will whet your appetite as you begin thinking about the important task of biblical integration. Having worked through the above principles, we now turn to the task of analyzing and engaging culture.

The culture in which we live, move, and have our being bombards us with images and ideas, especially through such mediums as social media, T.V., movies, and music. We're often hit from every angle with contrary ideas. How, then, are Christians to engage these ideas from a Christian point of view? How are we to think Christianly about the arts and culture?

Francis Schaeffer, in his short, but important book, *Art and the Bible*, outlines four criteria for evaluating art, no matter the platform. The first criterion is technical excellence. For example, when we study art, say, painting, we evaluate it based on the skill of the artist. What kinds of color or forms did the artist use?[21] What specific techniques does the piece of art display. Now, there's a wide variety of technique, style, and form in various artforms. But why is this important for Christians to consider? Here, I think Schaeffer hits the nail on its head.

> We are not being true to the artist as a man if we consider his art work junk simply because we differ with his outlook on life. Christian schools, Christian parents and Christian pastors often have turned off young people at just this point. Because the schools, the pastors and the parents did not make a distinction between technical excellence and content, the whole of much great art has been rejected by scorn or ridicule. Instead, if the artist's technical excellence is high, he is to be praised for this, even if we differ with his worldview. Man must be treated fairly as man. Technical excellence is, therefore, an important criterion.[22]

Schaeffer's second criterion is validity. Here, he means, is the artist being true to one's own worldview and to the self, or is the work done for some other reason? We can think of many artists who do their craft simply for material gain or for praise and glory—including those who practice the art of preaching.[23]

The third and fourth criteria deal with content. Does the artist's worldview come through (criterion three), and how well is it integrated into the artwork (criterion four)? Insightfully, Schaeffer stresses that every artwork has a worldview, whether the artist knows it or not.

> Some artists may not know that they are consciously showing forth a world view. Nonetheless, a world view usually does show through. Even those works which were constructed under the principle of art for art's sake often imply a world view. Even the world view that there is no meaning is a message. In any case, whether

---

[21]Francis A. Schaeffer, *Art and the Bible* (Downers Grove, IL: InterVarsity Press, 1973), 41-42.

[22]Ibid., 42.

[23]Ibid., 42-43.

the artist is conscious of the world view or not, to the extent that it is there it must come under the judgment of the Word of God.[24]

Intentionally or unintentionally, art displays a message. No art is neutral! As Schaeffer rightly points out, all art work must be evaluated and scrutinized by God's Word—even so-called "Christian" art. We must tread carefully, here. Just because something has the label "Christian" doesn't mean that it's inherently so. Unfortunately, Christians are often influenced by false ideologies, and these ideologies make their way into the cultural pieces they produce.

As we begin thinking Christianly about art and culture, we need to take up the habit of asking the right kinds of questions. Below is a sample of practical questions that may aid in the task of analyzing the theology and worldview of the cultural piece in question.

What does the author, artist, or work say about creation or human origins?

What does the author, artist, or work say about the created order?

What does the author, artist, or work tell us about the fallen state of humanity? What needs redeeming?

What does the author, artist, or work say about truth, meaning, and purpose in the world?

What does the author, artist, or work say about human nature or the rights and responsibilities of the individual?

What major worldviews or ideologies are prevalent within the work? What is the author or artist's worldview? What ideologies are being promoted?

What key theological themes are prevalent (e.g., providence, humanity, salvation, sin)?

How have those theological themes been represented, and how are they different from what we see in Christian theology and Scripture?

Theology, Integration, and Conclusion

This final chapter has taken up the challenge of helping Christians integrate their faith into daily practice. It places focus on key principles for integration that may be integrated into various disciplines. Moreover, this chapter provides practical steps for engaging and analyzing culture.

It is my earnest prayer that you walk away from this book seeing theology as much more than some academic pie-in-the-sky discipline or an intellectual pursuit. What we believe, what we feel (attitudes), and what we do has theological

---

[24]Ibid., 44.

ramifications. Everything is essentially theological! May you continually grow in your love for God as you pursue theology.

Doxology

[25] Now to him who is able to strengthen you according to my gospel and the preaching of Jesus Christ, according to the revelation of the mystery that was kept secret for long ages [26] but has now been disclosed and through the prophetic writings has been made known to all nations, according to the command of the eternal God, to bring about the obedience of faith— [27] to the only wise God be glory forevermore through Jesus Christ! Amen. (Rom 16:15-17)

he who is the blessed and only Sovereign, the King of kings and Lord of lords, [16] who alone has immortality, who dwells in unapproachable light, whom no one has ever seen or can see. To him be honor and eternal dominion. Amen. (1 Tim 6:15-16)

[24] Now to him who is able to keep you from stumbling and to present you blameless before the presence of his glory with great joy, [25] to the only God, our Savior, through Jesus Christ our Lord, be glory, majesty, dominion, and authority, before all time and now and forever. Amen. (Jude 24-25)

Selected Bibliography

Alston, William, "A Philosopher's Way Back to Faith." In *God and the Philosophers: The Reconciliation of Faith and Reason,* edited by Thomas V. Morris, 19-31. Oxford University Press, 1996.

Aristotle. "Nicomachean Ethics." In *Greek Philosophy: Thales to Aristotle,* edited by Reginald E. Allen, 262-374. New York: The Free Press, 1966.

Athanasius. *On the Incarnation.* Edited by Cliff Lee. Lexington, KY: Paradorx Media, 2007.

Backus, William and Marie Chapian. *Telling Yourself the Truth: Find Your Way Out of Depression, Anxiety, Fear, Anger, and Other Common Problems by Applying the Principles of Misbelief Therapy.* Bloomington, MN: Bethany House Publishing, 2000.

Bauckham, Richard. *Jesus and the God of Israel: God Crucified and Other Studies on the New Testament's Christology of Divine Identity.* Grand Rapids, MI: Wm. B. Eerdmans Publishing Co., 2008.

Beck, W. David, ed. *Opening the American Mind: The Integration of Biblical Truth in the Curriculum of the University.* Grand Rapids, MI: Baker Publishing Group, 1991.

Beilby, James K. *Thinking About Christian Apologetics: What It Is and Why We Do It.* Downers Grove, IL: InterVarsity Press, 2001.

Berkhof, Louis. *Systematic Theology.* New Combined ed. Grand Rapids, MI: Wm B. Eerdmans Publishing Co., 1996.

Bock, Darrell L. *Recovering the Real Lost Gospel: Reclaiming the Gospel as Good News.* Nashville, TN: Broadman and Holman, 2010.

Boyd, Gregory A. *Benefit of the Doubt: Breaking the Idol of Certainty.* Grand Rapids, MI: Baker Books, 2013.

Clark, David K. *Dialogical Apologetics: A Person-Centered Approach to Christian Defense.* Grand Rapids, MI: Baker, 1993.

_____. *To Know and Love God.* Wheaton, IL: Crossway Books, 2003.

Clifford, Ross and Philip Johnson. *The Cross is Not Enough: Living as Witnesses to the Resurrection.* Grand Rapids, MI: Baker Books, 2012.

Copan, Paul. *That's Just Your Interpretation: Responding to Skeptics Who Challenge Your Faith.* Grand Rapids, MI: Baker Books, 2001.

Cosgrove, Mark P. *Foundations of Christian Thought: Faith, Learning, and the Christian Worldview.* Grand Rapids, MI: Kregel, 2006.

Craig, William Lane. *The Existence of God and the Beginning of the Universe.* San Bernardino, CA: Here's Life Publishers, 1979.

Crosby, Donald A. *Nature as Sacred Ground: A Metaphysics for Religious Naturalism*. Reprinted ed. Albany, NY: State University of New York Press, 2016.

Cullmann, Oscar. *The Earliest Christian Confessions*. Translated by J. K. S. Reid. London: Lutterworth Press, 1949.

Davis, Stephen T. *God, Reason and Theistic Proofs*. Grand Rapids, MI: Wm B. Eerdmans Publishing Company, 1997.

Easwaren, Kkanth, trans. *Bhagavad Gita, The*. 2nd. ed. Canada: Nilgiri Press, 2007.

Eckel, Mark. *The Whole Truth: Classroom Strategies for Biblical Integration*. Chicago, IL: Xulon Press, 2003.

Erhman, Bart D. *God's Problem: How the Bible Fails to Answer Our Most Important Questions—Why We Suffer*. New York: HaperOne, 2008.

Erickson, Millard J. *The Word Became Flesh: A Contemporary Incarnational Christology*. Grand Rapids, MI: Baker Books, 1991.

"*exousia.*" In *The Lexham Analytic Lexicon to the Greek New Testament*, 2nd Revised ed. Logos Bible Software, 2011.

Geisler, Norman L. *Systematic Theology: God and Creation*, vol. 2. Minneapolis, MN: Bethany House Publishers, 2003.

Geisler, Norman L. and Patrick Zukeran. *The Apologetics of Jesus: A Caring Approach to Dealing with Doubters*. Grand Rapids, MI: Baker Books, 2009.

Geisler, Norman L. and William D. Watkins. *Perspectives: Understanding and Evaluating Today's World Views*. San Bernandino, CA: Here's Life Publishers, 1984.

Groothuis, Douglas, *Christian Apologetics: A Comprehensive Case for Biblical Faith* (Downers Grove, IL: InterVarsity Press, 2011.

Guinness, Os. *God in the Dark: The Assurance of Faith Beyond a Shadow of Doubt*. Wheaton, IL: Crossway, 1996.

Habermas, Gary R. *Dealing with Doubt*. Chicago, IL: Moody Press, 1990.

_____. "Evidential Apologetics." In *Five Views on Apologetics*, edited by Steven B. Cowan, 92-121. Grand Rapids, MI: Zondervan, 2000.

_____. *The Risen Jesus and Future Hope*. Lanham, MD: Rowman and Littlefield Publishers, 2003.

_____. *The Thomas Factor*. Nashville, TN: Broadman and Holman Publishers, 1999.

Harris, Paul. *Elements of Pantheism: A Spirituality of Nature and the Universe*. 3rd ed. CreateSpace Independent Publishing, 2013.

Hasker, William. *Metaphysics: Constructing a World View*. Downers Grove, IL: InterVarsity Press, 1983.

Heiser, Michael S. *The Unseen Realm: Recovering the Supernatural Worldview of the Bible*. Bellingham, WA: Lexham Press, 2015.

Hiebert, Paul G. *Transforming Worldviews: An Anthropological Understanding of How People Change*. Grand Rapids, MI: Baker Academic, 2008.

Hindson, Ed. "Cults, Characteristics of." In *The Popular Encyclopedia of Apologetics: Surveying the Evidence for the Truth of Christianity*, edited by Ed

Hindson and Ergun Caner, 158-161. Eugene, OR: Harvest House Publishers, 2008.

Holcomb, Justin S. *Know the Heretics.* Grand Rapids, MI: Zondervan, 2014.

Holmes, Arthur F. *All Truth is God's Truth.* Downers Grove, IL: InterVarsity Press, 1977.

_____. *Contours of a Worldview.* Grand Rapids, MI: William B. Eerdmans Publishing, 1983.

Howard-Snyder, Frances. "Christianity and Ethics." In *Reasons for the Hope Within,* edited by Michael J. Murray. 375-398. Grand Rapids, MI: William B. Eerdmans, 1999.

Hurtado, Larry W. *How On Earth Did Jesus Become a God?: Historical Questions about Earliest Christian Devotion to Jesus.* Grand Rapids, MI: Wm. B. Eerdmans Publishing Co, 2005.

_____. *Lord Jesus Christ: Devotion to Jesus in Earliest Christianity.* Grand Rapids, MI: Wm. B. Eerdmans Publishing Co., 2005.

Johnston, Gordon H. Genesis 1 and Ancient Egyptian Creation Myths. *Bibliotheca Sacra* 165, no. 2 (April-June 2008): 178-194.

Koukl, Greg. *Tactics: A Game Plan for Discussing Your Christian Convictions.* Grand Rapids, MI: Zondervan, 2009.

Lewis, C. S. *Mere Christianity.* New York: HaperSanFrancisco, 1980.

Licona, Michael R. "I'm a Doubting Thomas." https://www.risenjesus.com/im-doubting-thomas, July 18, 2014.

Longnecker, Richard N. "Christological Materials in the Early Christian Communities." In *Contours of Christology in the New Testament.* Ed. Richard N. Longnecker, 47-78. Grand Rapids, MI: William B. Eerdmans Publishing Company, 2005.

MacArthur, John, Jr. *Found: God's Will: Find the Direction and Purpose God Wants for Your Life.* Revised ed. Colorado Springs, CO: Victor, 1977.

McDermott, Gerald R. and Harold A. Netland. *A Trinitarian Theology of Religions: An Evangelical Proposal.* New York: Oxford University Press, 2014.

McGrath, Alister. *Doubting: Growing Through the Uncertainties of Faith.* Downers Grove, IL: InterVarsity Press, 2006.

_____. *The Christian Theology Reader.* 4th ed. Malden, MA: Wiley-Blackwell, 2011.

Meister, Chad V. *Building Belief: Constructing Faith from the Ground Up.* Grand Rapids, MI: Baker Books, 2006.

Melick, Richard R. *Philippians, Colossians, Philemon,* vol. 32, The New American Commentary. Nashville, TN: Broadman and Holman Publishers, 1991.

Miller, Johnny V. and John M. Soden, *In the Beginning . . . We Misunderstood: Interpreting Genesis 1 in Its Original Context.* Grand Rapids, MI: Kregel Publications, 2012.

Moreland, J. P. *Love Your God with All Your Mind: The Role of Reason in the Life of the Soul.* Colorado Springs, CO: NavPress, 1997.

_____. "Philosophy." In *Opening the American Mind: The Integration of Biblical Truth in the Curriculum of the University*, edited by W. David Beck, 47-66. Grand Rapids, MI: Baker Book House, 1991.

_____. *The Kingdom Triangle: Recover the Christian Mind, Renovate the Soul, Restore the Spirit's Power*. Grand Rapids, MI: Zondervan, 2007.

_____. "The Ontological Status of Properties." In *Naturalism: A Critical Analysis*, edited by William Lane Craig and J. P. Moreland, 67-109. New York: Routledge, 2000.

Morris, Thomas V. *Francis Schaeffer's Apologetic: A Critique*. Chicago: Moody Press, 1976.

Mother Teresa and Brian Kolodiejchuk. *Mother Teresa: Come Be My Light: The Private Writings of the "Saint of Calcutta."* Waterville, ME: Wheeler Publishing, 2008.

Mueller, Walt. *Understanding Today's Youth Culture: A Complete Guide for Parents, Teachers, and Youth Leaders*. Wheaton, IL: Tyndale, 1999.

Nash, Ronald H. *Faith and Reason: Searching for a Rational Faith*. Grand Rapids, MI: Zondervan, 1988.

_____. *Worldviews in Conflict: Choosing Christianity in a World of Ideas*. Grand Rapids, MI: Zondervan, 1992.

Naugle, David K. *Worldview: The History of a Concept* Grand Rapids, MI: William B. Eerdmans Publishing Co., 2002.

Neufeld, Vernon H. *The Earliest Christian Confessions*. Grand Rapids, MI: Wm. B. Eerdmans, 1963.

Oden, Thomas C. *Classic Christianity: A Systematic Theology*. New York: HaperOne, 1992.

Ortberg, John. *Faith and Doubt*. Grand Rapids, MI: Zondervan, 2008.

Piper, John. *Let the Nations Be Glad: The Supremacy of God in Missions*. 2nd ed. Grand Rapids, MI: Baker Academic, 2003.

Plantinga, Alvin. "Advice to Christian Philosophers: Preface." Reprinted from *Faith and Philosophy: Journal of the Society of Christian Philosophers* 1, no. 3 (October 1984): 253-271, accessed July 9, 2016, http://www. faithandphilosophy.com/article_advice.php

_____. *God, Freedom, and Evil*. Grand Rapids, MI: Wm B. Eerdmans Publishing Co., 1974.

Pyne, Robert A. *Humanity and Sin: The Creation, Fall, and Redemption of Humanity*. Nashville, TN: Word Publishing, 1999.

Quash, Ben. "Prologue." In *Heresies and How to Avoid Them: Why It Matters What Christians Believe*. Edited by Ben Quash and Michael Ward, 1-14.

Rue, Loyal. *Nature is Enough: Religious Naturalism and the Meaning of Life*. Albany, NY: State University of New York Press, 2011.

Schaefer, Francis. *Art and the Bible*. Downers Grove, IL: InterVarsity Press, 1973.

_____. *The God Who Is There*. 2nd ed. Downers Grove, IL: InterVarsity Press, 1982.

_____. *True Spirituality*. Wheaton, IL: Tyndale House Publishers, 1971.

Sire, James W. *Naming the Elephant*. Downers Grove, IL: InterVarsity Press, 2004.

_____. *The Universe Next Door*. 5th ed. Downers Grove, IL: InterVarsity Press, 2009.

Stone, Jerome A. *Religious Naturalism Today: The Rebirth of a Forgotten Alternative*. Albany, NY: State University of New York Press, 2009.

Storms, Sam. *Pleasure Evermore: The Life-Changing Power of Enjoying God*. Colorado Springs, CO: NavPress, 2000.

The Bellamy Brothers. "Lord Help Me Be the Kind of Person (My Dong Thinks I Am)" from the Album *Jesus is Coming*, Curb records, 2007.

Thiessen, Henry C. *Lectures in Systematic Theology*. Rev. ed. Reprint. Grand Rapids, MI: William B. Eerdmans, 2000.

James L. Snyder, ed. *Tozer on Worship and Entertainment*. Camp Hill, PA: WingSpreadPublishers, 1997.

Walker, James. "Occult." In *The Popular Encyclopedia of Apologetics: Surveying the Evidence for the Truth of Christianity*, edited by Ed Hindson and Ergun Caner, 367-371. Eugene, OR: Harvest House Publishers, 2008.

Walton, John H. *The Lost World of Genesis One: Ancient Cosmology and the Origins Debate*. Downers Grove, IL: InterVarsity Press, 2009.

Willard, Dallas. *Renovation of the Heart: Putting on the Character of Christ* (Colorado Springs, CO: NavPress, 2002.

_____. *The Divine Conspiracy: Rediscovering Our Hidden Life in God*. New York: HarperOne, 1997.

Wolters, Albert. M. *Creation Regained: Biblical Basics for a Reformational Worldview*. 2nd ed. Grand Rapids, MI: Wm B. Eerdmans Publishing Company, 2005.

Wolterstorff, Nicholas. *Lament for a Son*. Grand Rapids, MI: Wm B. Eerdmans Publishing Co., 2001.

_____. *Reason Within the Bounds of Religion*. 2nd ed. Reprint. Grand Rapids, MI: Wm. B. Eerdmans Publishing Co., 1999.

Wright, N. T. *After You Believe: Why Christian Character Matters*. New York: HarperOne, 2010.

_____. *Evil and the Justice of God*. Downers Grove, IL: InterVarsity Press, 2006.

Yancey, Philip. *Disappointment with God: Three Questions No One Asks Aloud*. Grand Rapids, MI: Zondervan, 1997.

_____. *Where is God When It Hurts*. Grand Rapids, MI: Zondervan, 2002.

Zuck, Roy B. "The Role of the Holy Spirit in Hermeneutics." In *Bibliotheca Sacra* 141 (1984): 120-129, accessed July 26, 2017, https://biblicalstu-dies.org.uk/article_spirit_zuck.html.

CPSIA information can be obtained
at www.ICGtesting.com
Printed in the USA
LVOW13s1547170118

563093LV00003B/325/P